Not so very long ago
(Or was it years before?)
I opened up a storybook
The way I open up a door.

Not So Very Long Ago

Not so very long ago
(Just the turning of a page!)
I stepped into a storybook
The way I step onto a stage.

Not so very long ago
(It was just yesterday.)
I lived inside a storybook
A hundred worlds away.
                    -Dawn Watkins

Reading 3 Part B
for Christian Schools®
Second Edition

Bob Jones University Press, Greenville, South Carolina 29614

NOTE: The fact that materials produced by other publishers may be referred to in this volume does not constitute an endorsement of the content or theological position of materials produced by such publishers. Any references and ancillary materials are listed as an aid to the student or the teacher and in an attempt to maintain the accepted academic standards of the publishing industry.

READING 3B for Christian Schools™
Not So Very Long Ago
Second Edition

Produced in cooperation with the Bob Jones University School of Education and Bob Jones Elementary School.

for Christian Schools is a registered trademark of BJU Press.

© 1999 BJU Press
Greenville, South Carolina 29614
First Edition © 1982 BJU Press

Printed in the United States of America

ISBN 1-59166-632-5

15 14 13 12 11 10 9 8 7 6 5 4 3 2 1

Contents

Treasures

A New Land

Creatures Great and Small

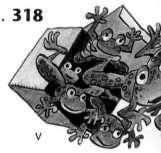

Acknowledgments

A careful effort has been made to trace the ownership of selections included in this textbook in order to secure permission to reprint copyright material and to make full acknowledgment of their use. If any error or omission has occurred, it is purely inadvertent and will be corrected in subsequent editions, provided written notification is made to the publisher.

Houghton Mifflin Company: Glossary material based on the lexical database of the *Children's Dictionary,* copyright © 1981 Houghton Mifflin Company. No part of this book may be reproduced or transmitted in any form or by any means, electronic or mechanical, including photocopying and recording, or by any information storage or retrieval system, except as may be expressly permitted by the 1976 Copyright Act or with prior written permission from both Houghton Mifflin Company and Bob Jones University Press.

"André" Copyright © 1956 by Gwendolyn Brooks Blakely. Used by permission of HarperCollins Publishers.
"Forgiven" from *Now We Are Six* by A. A. Milne. Copyright 1927 by E. P. Dutton, renewed © 1955 by A. A. Milne. Used by permission of Dutton Children's Books, a division of Penguin Books USA Inc.
"Lullaby" from *Collected Poems* by Robert Hillyer. Copyright 1933 and renewed 1961 by Robert Hillyer. Copyright © 1961 by Robert Hillyer. Reprinted by permission of Alfred A. Knopf Inc.
"Sunning" Copyright 1933, copyright renewed © 1973 by Martha K. Tippett. Used by permission of HarperCollins Publishers.

Design by Dan Van Leeuwen. Cover and title page by Holly Gilbert.
Unit openers illustrated by Paula Cheadle.

Photo Credits

The following agencies and individuals have furnished materials to meet the photographic needs of this textbook. We wish to express our gratitude to them for their important contribution.

Corel Corporation
Beverly Factor
The Greenville News

Breck P. Kent
Dan Nedrelo
PhotoDisc, Inc.

Simon and Schuster
U.S. Army

Just Plain Snaky
Breck P. Kent 77; © Dan Nedrelo 78, 79, 80, 81, 82

News About Ads
The Greenville News 142; Simon and Schuster 142 *(The Boston Newsletter* and *The Kansas City Star); PhotoDisc, Inc. 143

The Web Weavers
Corel Corporation 269; PhotoDisc, Inc. 266, 267, 268

Friends of the Prairie
Breck P. Kent 114, 115, 116, 117, 119; PhotoDisc, Inc. 118

What About Dolphins
Corel Corporation 272, 273, 274; © 1999 Beverly Factor 275; PhotoDisc, Inc. 276, 277; U.S. Army, photo by Specialist Eduardo Guajardo 278

Treasures

The Best Kind of Love

Eileen M. Berry
illustrated by John Roberts

Tortillas

Ana sat on the floor in the room she shared with Rosalina, watching her sister brush her long, black hair. "Are you excited about tonight?" she asked.

Rosalina shook her hair out behind her, and it fell like a dark, shiny blanket over her shoulders. "I can hardly wait." She did a little dance on her tiptoes. "All the family will be here, and some of my friends from school."

"Do you think my hair will be long and thick like yours when I'm your age?" Ana asked.

But Rosalina didn't hear. She hurried past Ana. "Mama! We still need to fix the hem on my dress."

"You'll have to do it, Rosalina," Mama called. "I'm busy with the cooking."

Rosalina rushed back into the room. She almost stumbled over Ana. "Ana, don't you have something to do?" Her voice was cross. "I wish we had a bigger house. Then I could have my own room."

Ana stood up without a word. She headed for the kitchen where Mama was.

"Here is some money." Mama pressed coins into Ana's hand. Ana leaned close to the pans on Mama's stove and breathed deeply, smelling spices. "Please go buy some tortillas from Señora Gomez and take your brother with you. Rosalina and I have much work to do."

Ana smiled at Mama. Only a few days ago, buying tortillas was Rosalina's job. But today Rosalina was celebrating her *quince años*, her fifteenth birthday. That meant she was no longer a child. And Mama said fifteen-year-old *señoritas* had bigger responsibilities than buying tortillas.

Ana ran outside.
She dropped the coins into
her right pocket and looked up the street. Juan was
running and dodging at the top of the hill, playing
with the dog, Chico. "Juan, let's go!" she called.

Juan raced down the hill, his hair bouncing like
flapping blackbird wings. His sandals made loud
slaps on the dirt. Chico outran him and pranced
around Ana's legs. Ana couldn't help laughing.

On the way to the market, Ana counted the coins
Mama had given her. "We will buy the tortillas with
this money," she said. She reached into her left pocket
and took out a few more coins. "And this," she said,
"is the money I've been saving to buy Rosalina's
birthday present."

Juan's eyes widened till they were big and round like saucers of hot chocolate. "Where'd you get it?"

Ana smiled. "Mama let me have some of the flower money because I helped with the garden," she said. "Juan, I'm going to buy Rosalina the perfect present."

"What will you buy?" Juan trotted to keep up with Ana's quick steps.

"I don't know yet. But it has to be perfect."

"Why does it have to be perfect?"

"Because it's for Rosalina's *quince años*. I want her to like my present best of all."

"Why does she have to like yours best?"

Ana didn't answer for a moment. "Because—because if she likes my present, she'll like *me,* that's why."

Juan tugged on her arm. "What do you mean, Ana? She likes you! I know she does. What do you mean?"

Ana sighed. "Juan, you ask too many questions."

The Ribbon

Ana held Juan's hand as they hurried through the market. Crates held brightly colored fruits and vegetables. Vendors called out the names of their wares.

Just ahead was Señora Gomez's stand. People called Señora Gomez the *tortillera*. Ana could see her kneading a large, white mound of dough and flashing her wide smile as she chatted with a customer.

Something sparkled off to Ana's left. She turned to see rows of jewelry displayed on a table. She pulled Juan to a halt and hesitated, thinking of Rosalina. She touched a gold chain.

"Very lovely, yes?" asked the pretty lady behind the table. Her hair hung in a long, dark braid over one shoulder. As long as Rosalina's, Ana thought. The lady had woven a silky white ribbon with threads of gold into the braid. The ends of the ribbon were tied in a knot at the bottom of the braid.

Ana looked down at the chain. "It is pretty," Ana said. "I want to buy the perfect present for my sister. She'll be fifteen."

"Ah. A special day in a young girl's life."

The lady held up a string of red painted beads.

"How much?" asked Ana.

"Seven pesos."

Ana shook her head slowly. "I have only three," she said. "What about hair jewelry?"

"I have barrettes," said the lady. "Gold, silver, some with pearls, some with jewels. Not real, but very beautiful. You can buy them for three pesos."

Ana watched the lady as she turned her head. The sun caught the gold threads in the ribbon, and it sparkled. "What about one like you have in your hair?" asked Ana.

The lady smiled. "My ribbons are expensive," she said. "I could not sell you one for less than five pesos. I'm sorry."

Ana looked at the coins in her hand, counting them again. Juan tugged on her other arm. "Ana, can't you buy a barrette? I want to go to Señora Gomez's."

"Just a minute, Juan." Ana thought how well the ribbon would match Rosalina's white dress for the party. It was the perfect present.

She glanced up at Señora Gomez again. The *tortillera* caught her eye and waved. "*Holá,* Ana and Juan!" she called. "Your sister must be excited for her *quince años* tonight! My Maria can hardly wait to come to the party."

Ana waved back. "*Holá,* Señora Gomez." She watched the señora roll a section of the dough out flat.

Ana looked down at the ribbon again. She dropped her three pesos on the table. Then she reached into her right pocket and counted out two more pesos. She plunked them down on the pile.

Juan gasped loudly. "Ana! You can't give away the tortilla money! Mama will be—"

"Hush, Juan," said Ana. She lifted her chin and said to the lady, "I'll take the ribbon, please. One just like yours."

The Perfect Present

Juan and Chico ran ahead of Ana on the way home. Ana dragged her feet a little. Every time she looked at the shiny ribbon in her hand, she felt a little prickle somewhere inside.

Mama was waiting for her at the door. Ana could tell that Juan had already been there.

"Young lady, come into the house," said Mama. "We need to talk."

Ana lowered her head as she approached. Mama did not ask where the tortillas were. She pointed to the couch. Ana sat down, and Mama sat down beside her. She took the ribbon from Ana's hand and ran it through her strong, brown fingers.

"Why is this ribbon so important?" Mama asked. Her voice was quieter than Ana had expected.

Ana's eyes burned. She blinked and swallowed,

but two tears spilled over anyway. "It's for Rosalina," she said. She thought that her voice sounded different—rushed and breathless. "I'm always in her way. She wishes she had her own room. I—I just wanted her to like me better." She put her head down in her hands and felt more tears drip through her fingers.

Mama waited and waited. Ana heard a bird twittering outside. She even heard a bee buzzing around the garden just beyond the open window. Ana finally looked up at Mama.

Mama was watching her. "And did you think, my dear little one, that love is something you can buy?"

Ana leaned against Mama and felt strong arms go around her. Mama stroked her hair with long, gentle strokes. "It was foolish to spend money that was not yours," Mama said. Her voice was soft but firm. "It was foolish to fail others who were counting on you."

Mama pulled away a little to look at Ana. "But most of all, Ana, it was foolish to believe that another's love for you depends on what you do. The best kind of love—well, it loves *just because.* And Rosalina loves you very, very much, my little Ana."

Ana glanced toward the room where Rosalina sat sewing. Then she brushed her hand across her eyes. When she spoke, her voice came out in a whisper. "Mama, may I keep the ribbon? To give to Rosalina? I'll pay you the extra."

Mama cradled Ana's chin in her hand. "You may keep the ribbon. I will take the cost from your flower money next time. And you must promise never to let this happen again."

Ana nodded. Her breath caught in a little sob.

"Now, go." Mama winked. "Go talk to your sister."

Ana went into the bedroom. Rosalina looked up and grinned. "Hello, little sister."

Suddenly Ana felt like smiling again. "I brought you something. It's a present for your *quince años*."

She held out the ribbon, and Rosalina's eyes opened wide. "Ana, it's beautiful, beautiful, beautiful!" she sang out. "I'll wear it tonight." She jumped up and gave Ana a hug. Then she held her away. "You paid a high price for this, Ana. But you're right—it's the perfect present."

Ana frowned up at her. "How did you know?"

Rosalina's eyes sparkled. Then her laughter bubbled out. "We have a little brother who keeps no secrets," she said. She took Ana's arms and danced her around in a circle. "I love you, little sister."

Then she turned, grabbed something from a jar by her bed, and dropped some coins in Ana's hand. "Here—Uncle Ramon sent money for my *quince años*." She gave Ana a playful swat. "Now, go buy the tortillas."

God Provides

Ruth Brail

illustrated by
Mary Ann Lumm

(taken from I Kings 17:8-16)

When Ahab became king, he did more to provoke the Lord God of Israel than all the kings of Israel that were before him. So the Lord sent Elijah, the prophet, before Ahab to tell him that neither rain nor dew would fall until he, Elijah, announced it. And the Lord hid Elijah from Ahab's fury by the brook Cherith and sent ravens to feed him. When the brook dried up, the Lord sent Elijah to Zarephath, where a widow gave him food and shelter. In this way, the Lord provided for His servant Elijah.

Heat pressed down on the dry land like a blanket, smothering the thirsty ground. Elijah pulled his cloak of camel's hair over his head to protect himself from the burning sun. In the distance he could see the walls of Zarephath.

"There will be water and food waiting for me," Elijah thought as he shook the dust from his sandals and garments. "God has said so."

As he came closer to the city, he saw a woman gathering sticks. She was dressed in the clothes of a widow. "Ah," thought Elijah. "She must be the woman of whom God spoke."

Raising his voice, he called, "I have traveled for many days without much water. Fetch me, I pray thee, a little water in a vessel, that I may drink."

The woman turned to get some water for Elijah. She had not gone far when Elijah called to her again.

"Bring me, I pray thee, a morsel of bread in thine hand."

She stopped and turned back to Elijah. "I am sorry, but I have not one cake. I have only a handful of meal in the bottom of my barrel and a little oil in a jar. I am gathering these sticks so that I may go in and cook for myself and my son. We were going to eat our last meal and die."

"Do not be afraid," said Elijah, speaking to the woman kindly. "Do as you planned, but first make me a little cake. Then bake cakes for yourself and your son. For the Lord God of Israel has said that your barrel of meal shall not be empty, nor shall the jar of oil be used up, until the day that the Lord sends rain upon the earth."

The woman picked up her sticks and hurried to do as Elijah had told her. When she made Elijah's cake, oil and meal were still left!

And in all the years of the drought, the jar of oil was never empty, and there was always enough meal for Elijah, the widow, and her son.

For three years the drought lasted. The grass disappeared from the hillsides, and the fields became wastelands. Although Ahab searched for Elijah so that he could slay him, Elijah was not to be found. He was safe in the house of the widow, waiting on the Lord.

A Jar of Oil

Milly Howard

illustrated by Mary Ann Lumm

In Bible times, oil was both a necessity and a luxury. Olive oil could be found in the home of every family, from the richest queen to the poor widow who helped Elijah.

The oil was expensive and took a long time to make. The best oil came from olives that were picked just after they ripened and before they turned black. If the olives were picked too green, the oil would be bitter. If the olives were picked too ripe, the oil would be rancid.

Olives were crushed with a heavy stone to remove the oil. When the stone first broke the skin, much oil came from the pulp. This first oil was of the highest grade. More pressing produced oil of a cheaper grade.

Used in cooking, olive oil prevented meat or bread from sticking to the pan. Sometimes the oil was mixed with flour or meal to make bread dough or cakes similar to those that the widow fed Elijah.

The lamps in most houses burned with a wick that soaked in a small clay bowl of olive oil. In the tabernacle the golden lampstand burned pure olive oil from small cups.

Olive oil was also thought to promote healing. Cuts and scrapes were rubbed with the oil, and wealthy people took baths in warm olive oil. Women rubbed the oil into their skin to keep it soft. The kings of Israel were anointed with the finest olive oil.

Oil in Bible times was used every day in many different ways. Because it was so important to everyday life, anyone who had large amounts of oil was thought to be prosperous and to have great joy.

Elly's Secret

Gail Fitzgerald / illustrated by Steven Patricia

In the fall of 1864, Sherman began his march to the sea. Having destroyed the railroad to the rear, he was dependent on the countryside for supplies. His Union troops swept a sixty-mile-wide path as they looted and burned their way across Georgia. Bands of foragers raided outlying plantations to provide food for the huge army and destroyed anything that might be left to sustain the Confederacy.

A Secret Shared

The late November morning of 1864 made no promise of being unusual. If anything, it was quiet— too quiet. Eight-year-old Elly Pritchard wandered through the strangely bare parlor and walked out onto the side porch. Down by the cotton barn she caught a glimpse of her brothers as they dashed quickly into the shadowed doorway.

"Humph," she thought to herself. "Probably hiding something else."

Last week when the news had come that the Yankees were in Georgia, Elly was sick in bed. Everyone had rushed around hiding anything that was of value. Frustrated, Elly had watched from her bedroom window, shouting questions to all who hurried by. Her hoarse shouts had quickly brought Mother and Pearl to tuck her back in bed with orders not to get out again. Elly had watched helplessly as the silver pitcher and candlesticks were whisked from her room, along with the filigree music box Papa had sent her from Atlanta.

When Elly was well and downstairs again, her questions were fended off with, "Hush, child, the less you know the better."

But this morning Elly had asked so many questions that her mother had told her a secret. It was a much better secret than where something was hidden. Elly hugged her doll tightly as she set off across the lawn to the cotton barn at the edge of the red clay fields. When she reached the barn, the doors were closed. Elly gave one of the doors a push, and it swung slowly inward, squeaking on its hinges. Elly stepped into the cool darkness.

"Tom! Jake! Where are you? I know you're in here!"

Jake's ten-month-old puppy, Bruiser, whined at
the foot of the loft ladder. Jake and Tom peeped
down through the cracks in the loft. "Go play, Elly.
We're busy."

"Please let me come up too!" Elly ran to the loft
ladder.

"Nope," said Jake. "We have too many secret
things up here. If we let you come up, they won't be
secrets anymore."

"That's right." Tom scrambled to his knees and started counting on his fingers. "Remember the time Father brought Jake a puppy for his birthday and you told? Or the time—"

Elly put her hands on her hips and narrowed her eyes. "Then I won't tell you the secret I just found out from Mother."

Tom glanced at his older brother and grinned. Then both boys looked at Elly, shrugged their shoulders, and said in unison, "We don't care." Jake swung his legs over the edge of the loft and pulled out his knife while Tom put his harmonica to his lips.

Elly sighed. It was such a good secret. The boys wouldn't be sitting around if they knew. Just thinking about the secret made Elly's feelings dance like the tune on Tom's harmonica.

She stooped over and petted Bruiser. If she told only two people, it would still be a secret, wouldn't it? Elly put her doll, Amanda Lyn, on the ladder and looked up at the boys. She licked her dry lips and burst out, "You would care if you knew that Father was coming home tonight!"

"He is?"

"For sure?" Jake and Tom were already scrambling down the ladder.

"Whoopee!" Both boys took off toward the house. Elly sighed. She had done it again. When would she learn not to tell secrets!

Bruiser, sensing the boys' excitement, leaped up, barking at Elly. Suddenly he grabbed Amanda Lyn and took off after the boys.

"Stop! Stop!" Elly ran after Bruiser and Amanda Lyn. At last, tired of the game, Bruiser gave Amanda Lyn a final shake. Glass beads scattered as he dropped the doll at Elly's feet.

With tears streaming down her cheeks, Elly picked up Amanda Lyn. The doll's blue dress was tattered and torn. Stuffing hung out where Bruiser's teeth had made a long rip. Sobbing, Elly cradled the doll in her arms and ran to Mother.

"There, there," said Mother, wiping away Elly's tears. "Let me see Amanda Lyn." Mother took the torn dress off and poked the stuffing back in. "Go get a new dress for Amanda Lyn and gather her beads while I sew her together."

Elly nodded and ran off. She looked in the closet, she hunted in the dresser, and she even searched under the bed. But Amanda Lyn's dress wasn't anywhere.

"Mother will know where it is," Elly thought to herself. She ran back and burst into the sewing room.

"Oh!" Her mouth dropped open. Mother was stuffing something that glittered into the hole in Amanda Lyn's back.

"Why are you putting your diamond necklace inside Amanda Lyn?"

Mother didn't say a word until she had sewn up the rip. Then she drew Elly close to her.

"When your father comes, he will take my jewelry to a bank in Savannah." Mother's serious gray eyes looked into Elly's blue ones. "Elly, Amanda Lyn will keep the jewels safe until tonight. It will be our secret—yours, mine, and Amanda Lyn's. Don't tell *anyone,* Elly!" She smiled and hugged Elly. "But remember, you and the boys are more precious to me than any jewels."

Elly nodded. The clattering of boys' boots in the hall kept her from saying anything.

"Mother, Mrs. Sully's mighty sick." Jake's face was flushed from running. "Her husband wants to know if you can come right away."

Mother began gathering up her things. "Jake, tell Pearl to fix some broth for me to take. Elly, put Amanda Lyn upstairs on your bed. Then go gather her beads and string them together. Now you children be good and obey Pearl while I'm gone."

A Secret Kept?

Late that afternoon Elly sat on the back porch, stringing Amanda Lyn's glass beads. "These beads almost look like diamonds. Amanda Lyn and I will pretend they are."

Elly tied the last knot and yawned. The sun warmed her back while the gentle breeze rustled the fall leaves as if whispering secrets.

"I've got a new secret too." Elly wiggled with delight. "But I'm not supposed to tell." She frowned. How in the world was she ever going to keep this important secret?

"Pearl's smart. I'll ask her." Elly ran upstairs and put the beads on Amanda Lyn. Then she ran down to the kitchen.

"Pearl, what do you do with a secret that's just itching to pop out?"

The old woman's chuckle filled the room. "Why, honey child, I just tell the Lord. He knows all the secrets of the world."

"Oh." Elly wandered back outside and sat down to think. It was comforting to know that the Lord knew Amanda Lyn's secret too. Elly hugged her doll closer.

Plop! An acorn fell from the tree, right onto her nose.

"Jake! You stop that!"

"Why?"

"I'm thinking."

"About what?"

"My new secret."

Jake dropped from the tree. "I'll let you see what's in my pocket if you'll tell me your secret."

Elly eyed his pocket, noticing a fairly large, interesting lump. But this time she did not need someone to share her secret. She already had Mother, Amanda Lyn, and the Lord.

Suddenly the sound of horses' hooves coming up the long avenue broke the stillness of the fall afternoon. Jake wasn't interested in the secret anymore.

"Father's home!" he shouted, disappearing around the corner of the house.

"Father's home!" Elly echoed and went running after him. Behind her she heard pounding footsteps which she recognized as Tom's. By the time Elly reached the front porch, she knew it wasn't Father that had come. Yankee soldiers were scattering throughout the plantation at the command of their captain. Horses whinnied, tossing their sweaty heads. Angry shouts came from the direction of the smokehouse.

"You won't find any hams there," she thought with sudden pleasure. Then her face sobered as soldiers appeared around the house, clutching struggling chickens and turkeys. Other soldiers on horseback were herding the servants away from the house.

An order was shouted. "Burn the cotton!" Elly clutched Amanda Lyn close as she saw the stricken look on Tom's and Jake's faces. "Their treasures are in the barn loft," she thought. Jake ran down the steps, only to be blocked by an officer galloping by.

"Jenkins!" the man called to the soldier running around the corner of the porch. "Take these children inside!"

"Yes, sir!" The soldier saluted, turned on his heel, and pointed inside. Tom grabbed Elly's hand and hurried her along behind Jake, who marched ahead of them like a soldier himself. Elly couldn't tell if Jake was scared or not. But Tom's hand was awfully clammy, and she felt her own heart beating like a drum. Elly bit her lip to keep from crying.

The soldier motioned the children into the parlor. Elly and Tom huddled close together on the couch. Jake scorned a seat, standing tall and straight.

The children watched in silent anger as the soldier went from table to table pulling open drawers and spilling their contents onto the floor. When he found nothing of value, he turned to the children. Elly shrank back at the look on his face.

"Where are your mother's jewels?" the soldier snarled, shifting his rifle in his hands.

Jake went white but didn't answer. The soldier strode across the room and grabbed Jake by his shirt.

"Where are they?" he shouted, shaking the boy.

"I don't . . . know," Jake said between clenched
teeth.

"Don't lie to me!" The soldier raised his hand as if
to cuff Jake.

Elly clutched Amanda Lyn. She knew where the jewels were, but it was a secret. Mother had said not to tell . . . but Mother wouldn't want Jake hurt! She jumped up. "He's telling the truth. He doesn't know where they are. I didn't tell him the secret."

The soldier relaxed his grip on Jake. A smile curled his lips. "Maybe you should tell the secret to me."

Elly nodded. "Amanda Lyn has the jewels."

"A mandolin? Where?"

Slowly Elly held up her doll. The soldier's greedy eyes lit up as he saw the shimmering beads around the doll's neck.

He grabbed the doll and tore the necklace off. When he held the necklace up to the light his face grew red. His back stiffened.

"Fakes!" he yelled, throwing the beads and the doll to the floor. His whole body shook with rage as he headed for Elly.

"Soldier!" A voice barked from the doorway.

The soldier froze and turned to face his officer. "Since when do we make war on children?" said the officer. "Take him outside," he said to the men behind him, "and mount up. There's a Confederate regiment to the south. Move!"

With loud shouts and the sound of clattering hooves, the Yankees were gone. The children could hear the servants trying to put out the fire.

"That was close." Jake picked up Amanda Lyn and handed her to Elly. "Thanks, Elly, but what . . ."

Tom headed for the door. "Come on, Jake! The barn's burning!"

The boys raced outside. Elly followed slowly, clutching Amanda Lyn. "I told the secret, but no one understood," she whispered. "Our secret is still safe!"

Elly's mother returned to find her home and children safe. The year's cotton harvest was lost, but enough food had been hidden to feed them through the remainder of the war. Elly's father did not come that night, nor the next, but Elly and Amanda Lyn kept their secret until he returned. The jewels that Elly had kept safe were later sold to provide food for the Pritchards and many of their friends during the hard years following the war.

Two Crooks and Two Heroes

Karen Wilt

*illustrated by Del Thompson
and Janet Davis*

Act I

Narrator: One hot Fourth of July, in the little town of Porcupine Hollow, more than just a parade was taking place. Our story begins at Mayor Setton's house. Travis Setton and his friend, Billy Bob, have been chosen to lead the Independence Day parade.

Travis: Bye, Mom and Dad. Wave to me from the grandstand!

Mrs. Setton: We'll make sure we see you!

Mayor Setton: I'll be right proud of you two today, carrying the flags. That's quite an honor.

Billy Bob: Yes sir, Mayor Setton.

Mrs. Setton: Run along the back way, boys, down Stray Cat Alley, so you won't have to cross any streets.

Travis: Yes, ma'am.

Billy Bob: Come on, Travis. We'll be late.

Narrator: The boys left the house and turned down the alley between Taylor's Hardware and Porcupine Hollow Bank.

Billy Bob: Mr. Taylor's closing his shop already.

Travis: The bank's closed too. But Uncle Clem must have forgotten to turn off the lights.

Billy Bob: Look, there's Uncle Clem's armored truck. I wonder why he parked it in the alley?

Travis: Probably so no one would sit on it during the parade.

Billy Bob: Uncle Clem is pretty smart.

Travis: Did you hear that? Something's inside Uncle Clem's truck.

Billy Bob: We'd better take a look. Give me a hand, and I'll peek through the window.

Travis: See anything, Billy Bob?

Billy Bob: It's Uncle Clem, tied up like a horsefly in a spider's web! Uncle Clem! How'd you get in there?

Uncle Clem: Ah, uh, uh . . .

Billy Bob: We'll get help. You just hold on.

Uncle Clem: Eh . . . ee . . . ou . . .

Billy Bob: Travis, you saw lights on in the bank, didn't you? I bet bank robbers did this!

Travis: You think they tied up Uncle Clem, locked him in the armored truck, and opened the safe?

Billy Bob: They're probably robbing the bank this second! Let's barricade the door so they can't get out!

Travis: If we stick this old crowbar through the door handles, they'll be stuck inside.

Billy Bob: Shhh! I hear them talking.

Narrator: Inside the bank two men were emptying the vault.

Shane: Grady, get those sacks of coins and put 'em by the door. I'll clean out the drawers up front.

Grady: Sure, boss. Easy as stealin' candy from a baby.

Shane: How much longer will that take you? We've got to get out of here.

Grady: Well, boss, them bags is plenty heavy. I can't tote them too fast. It'll probably take half an hour.

Shane: Half an hour? Move it! We need to be out of here before that parade blocks our getaway.

Grady: Sure, boss. I'll be done before then if you say so.

Shane: I say so!

Narrator: Outside the bank door, the two boys looked at each other, wide-eyed.

Billy Bob: Come on, Travis. We don't have much time.

Travis: Shhhh. Those two sure do *sound* tough, but just wait 'til Sheriff Ridgely gets his hands on them. They'll be two sorry criminals.

Billy Bob: Let's find Sheriff Ridgely before those crooks get us, or we'll be two sorry crook catchers locked up in the bank safe!

Act II

Narrator: Travis and Billy Bob raced through the alley. As they reached Main Street, the parade was just starting down the street. Mrs. Sullivan was hurrying along beside the band. Deputy Slim was walking with her, holding two flags.

Billy Bob: Travis, there's Deputy Slim.

Travis: Deputy Slim, Uncle Clem's been tied up and locked in his armored truck!

Billy Bob: Two robbers are stealing all the money in the bank!

Deputy Slim: Whooeeee, Sheriff Ridgely has been looking all over for you two. Two bank robbers are going to hold us up? And to think, I just dropped my paycheck off at the bank this morning. Come on; Sheriff Ridgely can't be far away.

Mrs. Sullivan: Boys, you're late! Get in your places. Here are your flags.

Deputy Slim: You hold the flags, boys; I'll find the sheriff.

Billy Bob: What should we do with these flags, Travis?

Travis: I don't know. We can't leave them.

Narrator: The two boys and Deputy Slim were swept along with the band. As they turned the corner, they saw the sheriff on the sidewalk, trying to look in both directions at once.

Billy Bob: There's the sheriff, Deputy Slim!

Band: Crash, boom, oompah, clang, clang, boom.

Deputy Slim: Sheriff Ridgely! The bank's being robbed! Stop the parade!

Sheriff Ridgely: What?

Travis: Uncle Clem's tied up in his armored truck!

Sheriff Ridgely: Lead the way, boys. The parade will have to wait.

Narrator: The boys turned up Stray Cat Alley, their flags waving in the breeze. The band followed, cymbals crashing, horns tooting.

Band: Oom, oompah, crash, clang.

Billy Bob: Oh, no, Travis. The parade is following us!

Narrator: Sheriff Ridgely clapped his hand to his head and groaned. Then he signaled for the band to stop playing. The parade followed them the rest of the way into the alley on tiptoe.

Travis: There's the armored truck, Sheriff. See the door to the bank? We stuck a crowbar in the handle to keep the robbers from breaking out.

Sheriff Ridgely: Good thinking, boys. All right, back up. We don't know if the robbers are armed.

Deputy Slim: Here they come now!

Narrator: The door of the bank rattled. Inside the bank someone grumbled loudly.

Shane: Grady, why did you lock this door? You knew we had to come back out this way. Now we'll have to break out like we broke in.

Grady: Boss, I didn't lock the door. It's stuck!

Sheriff Ridgely: Come out with your hands up!

Narrator: The sheriff removed the crowbar. Slowly the door opened, and the two crooks stepped out.

Shane: We're caught again!

Band: Crash, clang, oompah!

Grady: Boss, look! Do you think they'll let us watch the parade first?

Deputy Slim: Nope. It's to jail for you crooks. I'm sure Uncle Clem will want to thank Travis and Billy Bob. Let's untie him.

Sheriff Ridgely: Go ahead while I handcuff these two fellows.

Uncle Clem: Thank you, Travis and Billy Bob. You did a fine job. Give the flags to Deputy Slim and hop in my truck. I'll drive you to the grandstand. You're the heroes of the day!

Band: Clash, clang, oompah, pah.

Narrator: The band followed the slow-moving truck through the streets to the grandstand. There Billy

Bob and Travis took their places at the front of the line, holding the flags.

Mrs. Sullivan: Three cheers for Travis Setton and Billy Bob Moore!

Townsfolk: Hip, hip, hooray! Hip, hip, hooray! Hip, hip, hooray!

Mrs. Sullivan: Stand up tall, boys. Let those flags wave!

Mayor Setton: Come on up to the grandstand, boys. I'm as proud as a peacock. Catching bank robbers! Next thing I know one of you will be running for president of the United States.

Billy Bob: Yes sir, Mayor Setton.

Townsfolk: Hip, hip, hooray!

André

Gwendolyn Brooks

illustrated by Luvon Sheppard

I had a dream last night. I dreamed
I had to pick a Mother out.
I had to choose a Father too.
At first, I wondered what to do,
There were so many there, it seemed,
Short and tall and thin and stout.

But just before I sprang awake,
I knew what parents I would take.

And *this* surprised and made me glad:
They were the ones I always had!

Beautiful Feet

Ruth Brail / illustrated by Roger Bruckner

The age-old custom of binding feet to make them beautiful causes this Chinese lady to appreciate the Bible's description of "beautiful feet." Her tale is an adaptation of a true story that has often been told to encourage others in faithful witnessing.

The Mission School

Tired from packing, Ming-Chu sat down on the porch of the mission school. She smiled at the shouts of the children on the playground, remembering her own first years at the mission school. Her thoughts were interrupted by the sound of running feet.

"Ming-Chu! Watch out!"

Ming-Chu looked up as a ball bounced close to her feet. Reaching down, she picked up the ball and tossed it to the bright-eyed little girl who came racing after it. "Run," Ming-Chu called.

The little girl called back over her shoulder as she ran back to the playground. "Come and watch us, Ming-Chu!"

Ming-Chu followed the running child down the path, moving slowly and carefully in her tiny shoes.

At the edge of the playground, she stopped to watch the game.

Two leaders of the teams urged the children on to victory. One leader was the missionary, head of the mission school, and the other leader was a young Chinese man. Both men were special to Ming-Chu. The American missionary had been like a father to her during her years at the mission school, and the young Chinese was the man Ming-Chu was to marry. As the game ended, the two men walked toward her, arguing cheerfully.

"Just wait until tomorrow!" said the missionary as they stopped beside Ming-Chu.

"You hear him, Ming-Chu?" said the young Chinese. "Another day! Always another day!"

Ming-Chu smiled. "And I will not be here to see either of you win. It is hard to believe it is my last day at the mission school."

The missionary took her hand. "Now, Ming-Chu, this is not a time for sadness. You are returning home to prepare for your wedding."

The young man nodded. "I too will miss the mission school. But I am looking forward to a new life with you, Ming-Chu. The missionary has brought the gospel to us. Now we will give the gospel to others."

As Ming-Chu smiled up at him, the porters came down the trail, carrying a sedan chair. "It is time for me to go," she said. "I will return as swiftly as possible with my family."

When the porters stopped in front of them, the young man carefully helped Ming-Chu into the sedan chair. Then he warned the porters to take special care of Ming-Chu. "I want no harm to come to my bride to be."

Ming-Chu laughed. "We have made the trip often. I will return in one piece!"

"And in time for the wedding," the missionary said as the porters picked up the sedan chair.

"And in time for the wedding," Ming-Chu called back as the caravan began moving up the mountain trail.

Days later the caravan reached Ming-Chu's village. Children and neighbors crowded around the sedan chair as it moved slowly through the streets to Ming-Chu's house. Ming-Chu called greetings to her friends. Then the gates of her house were opened, and a servant appeared to take her to her eagerly waiting parents.

Early the next morning Ming-Chu's mother sent for the tailor. Soon material was spread across the room in a silken rainbow of bright colors.

The tailor carefully measured Ming-Chu for her wedding dress.

"Now the shoes," he said, spreading parchment on the floor. "What beautiful feet," he murmured as he traced Ming-Chu's feet on the parchment. "You must be very proud of such tiny feet."

Ming-Chu's mother beamed. "I bound her feet when she was just a baby. They are the smallest feet in the village, even smaller than my own."

Ming-Chu thought of the little girl back at the
mission school who had run so lightly after the ball.
What freedom the children had whose feet were not
bound!

Preparations continued for the wedding trip. Soon
the caravan was packed and ready to go. As Ming-Chu
and her family traveled across the mountains, she
watched eagerly for the first glimpse of the mission
school. At last they reached the last mountain pass.
There far below them lay the mission school.

"There it is!" called Ming-Chu to her parents. "We
are almost there!"

A Special Gift

Ming-Chu and her family were welcomed, and the wedding festivities began. After a week of joyful celebration, Ming-Chu's family returned to their village. Ming-Chu and her new husband prepared for their first trip together into the mountains of China.

"Thank you for everything you have done for us," the two young people told the missionary. "We will miss you and will think of you often."

"May God be with you," said the missionary.

"Good-bye," called the children as Ming-Chu and her husband started down the trail, Ming-Chu in her sedan chair carried by the porters and her husband walking alongside her.

That trip was the first of many. From village to village the young people went, carrying the gospel to the Chinese. In each village Ming-Chu's husband preached, and Ming-Chu taught the women from the Bible.

The women were delighted with Ming-Chu's tiny feet and came often to hear her teach. They began to look forward to the visits of the "lady with the beautiful feet," and many of them came to know Christ as their Savior.

Ming-Chu enjoyed the long walks over the mountains to the different villages. As her husband walked alongside the sedan chair, Ming-Chu would read the Bible aloud.

One day she was reading a passage from Romans: "How beautiful are the feet of them that preach the gospel of peace, and bring glad tidings of good things!" Ming-Chu closed her Bible and looked along the path. "I wish I could walk with you," she said to her husband.

"There are pebbles along the path," he answered. "What if you slip and fall?"

"I would be careful to lean on you," Ming-Chu replied wistfully.

Her husband hesitated, then stopped the caravan and let her walk slowly along the path. He held her arm firmly as she walked.

"I wish my feet had never been bound," Ming-Chu said sadly. "Then I could walk easily beside you, and we would not have to travel slowly because of my sedan chair."

"But Ming-Chu," replied her husband, "you have beautiful feet!"

"No," Ming-Chu said, "you have beautiful feet."

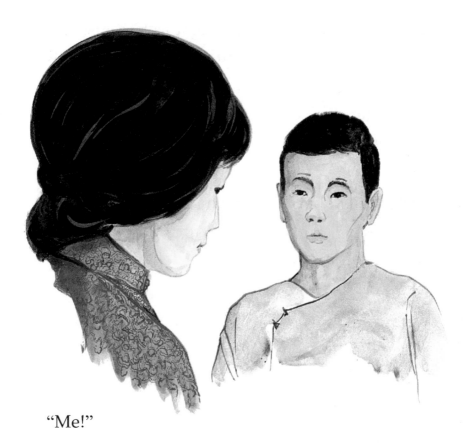

"Me!"

"Yes, you," Ming-Chu said tenderly. "The verse I just read says that the feet of those who carry the gospel to others are beautiful. That makes your feet beautiful, and mine are beautiful only because I help you, not because they are so tiny."

"I understand," said her husband. "But the Lord has used your tiny feet to bring many women to hear you teach. They come to marvel at your feet and stay to hear the gospel. The Lord uses what each of us has to further the gospel."

Ming-Chu thought for a moment as her husband helped her back into the sedan chair. "Do you know who else has beautiful feet?"

"The missionary," replied her husband. "He brought the gospel to us. Soon we will go back to visit him."

"I would like that very much," Ming-Chu replied.

But it was many years before they saw the missionary again. One day they received word that he was returning to the United States.

"We must go now," said Ming-Chu, "or we will never see him again."

"Yes, we will leave tomorrow," said her husband.

As Ming-Chu packed for the trip, she found her little silk wedding shoes in a tiny box. "Husband," she said, showing him the shoes, "these shoes remind me of the verse in Romans about beautiful feet. I would like to give the shoes to the missionary."

Her husband nodded. "The little shoes will make a fine gift of remembrance."

When Ming-Chu and her husband returned to the mission, they were joyfully met by their old friends. When at last they were able to sit down with the missionary alone, Ming-Chu gave him the little shoes.

She explained what beautiful feet now meant to her and asked the missionary, "Will you find some little girl in America who loves the Lord and give her these shoes? Perhaps my story will encourage her to carry the gospel to others as you have done."

When the missionary returned to America, he gave the tiny silk wedding shoes to an eight-year-old girl. She cherished the tiny shoes and never forgot the story of Ming-Chu's "beautiful feet." The girl grew up to serve the Lord faithfully in many ways. She kept the tiny shoes and often showed them to others. After she told Ming-Chu's story, she encouraged her listeners to be faithful in spreading the gospel so that they too might have beautiful feet.

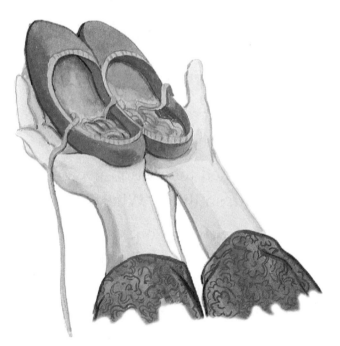

A Snake in the House

Milly Howard

illustrated by
John Roberts and Johanna Berg

A Pet for the Summer

"Dad! Dad!" The screen door slammed behind Lisa as she ran to the driveway.

Mr. Peroni stopped the station wagon. "What a welcome," he said, smiling. "What's going on?"

"Mom said I could keep one of the classroom pets for the summer if it's all right with you," Lisa said hurriedly. "We just have time to catch Mrs. Allen before she leaves."

"Hold on a minute." Mr. Peroni frowned. "Today's the last day of school. Why didn't we hear about this earlier?"

"I thought Paul Bartlett was going to keep Barney," Lisa replied, "and all the other animals were taken. Paul's parents decided to go away for the summer, so he called me a few minutes ago. If we hurry, we can get to the school in time."

"All right, let's go," Mr. Peroni said, reaching across to open the car door for Lisa. Lisa slid into the seat, and Mr. Peroni backed the car out of the driveway.

"Now you're sure it's okay with your mother?"

"Yes, sir. Mom just said I would have to take care of Barney myself." Lisa leaned forward, peering out the window.

Mr. Peroni slowed for the stop sign at Fifth and Oak Streets. "Do you know how to care for this Barney animal?"

"Oh, yes, sir," Lisa replied without taking her eyes from the road. "Snakes are easy to take care of anyway."

"Snakes?" Mr. Peroni stepped on the brake and turned to look at Lisa. "Snakes? Your mother agreed to let you keep a snake?"

"In the garage, not in the house," Lisa said hastily. "I promised to keep him in a cage in the garage."

Mr. Peroni shook his head, then turned left on Fifth Street. "Lisa, do you know why your mother is afraid of snakes?"

"She was bitten by a snake when she was little, wasn't she?"

"Yes. She was very sick, Lisa. She has been afraid of snakes ever since." Mr. Peroni turned onto Elm Street. "I want you to remember that and be careful with your snake."

"I will, Dad. Barney isn't poisonous. You know the school wouldn't let us keep a dangerous snake," Lisa said earnestly.

Mr. Peroni laughed. "I wouldn't think so."

He stopped the car in the school parking lot. "You run ahead and see if Mrs. Allen is still there. I'll park the car and catch up with you."

"Thanks, Dad!" Lisa slid out and slammed the door.

By the time Mr. Peroni reached the classroom, Lisa was hanging over a glass tank in the back. Mr. Peroni nodded to Mrs. Allen. "I see Lisa reached you in time. Looks like we'll have a guest for the summer."

"You don't know how glad I am to see you!" Mrs. Allen said. "No one wanted to take Barney. I didn't know what I was going to do."

"No one wanted a snake?" Mr. Peroni asked.

"Oh, the problem wasn't the children. It was the parents," she said, leading Mr. Peroni to the back. "A lot of people just don't care for boa constrictors."

"Boa . . ." Mr. Peroni coughed, leaning over Lisa's shoulder to look at the snake coiled in the heavy tank.

"He's just a baby boa, Dad," Lisa said. "Just look at him!"

"Lisa, did you tell your mother that Barney is a boa constrictor?"

Lisa looked up, startled. "I don't remember, Dad. I told her he was a snake and that he was a baby, but I don't remember if I said he was a boa or not. We always called him Barney here at school." She bit her lip and looked at Barney.

"I'll understand if you can't take Barney . . ." Mrs. Allen began.

"No," Mr. Peroni said, looking at Lisa's disappointed face. "Lisa said she would take good care of Barney, and I'm going to hold her to her word."

Lisa's head flew up. "You mean . . ."

"I mean we had better get Barney loaded before Mrs. Allen runs us out of here," Mr. Peroni said.

"Oh, boy!" Lisa took hold of one end of the tank. Mr. Peroni took the other end, and they carried the heavy tank to the station wagon.

When they got home, Mr. Peroni and Lisa carried Barney into the garage. Then Mr. Peroni went inside while Lisa made Barney comfortable. A little later Lisa's mother and father came out together.

Lisa looked up happily. "Come and look, Mom. Barney's looking the place over."

Mrs. Peroni came a few steps farther and peered at the cage. Barney's tongue flickered as he moved closer to the glass. Mrs. Peroni took a quick step backward. "Beautiful, isn't he?" she said quietly. "What's he doing?"

"Just smelling you," Lisa replied.

Mrs. Peroni gasped. "He can smell me?"

"Sure," Lisa said. "He puts his tongue out to test the air, then puts it on the roof of his mouth. That's the way he smells."

"Smells!" Mrs. Peroni backed away. "I think I'll go check on my cake."

Lisa watched her hurry back inside the house. "Don't you want to watch Barney climb up the tree branch?" she asked, disappointed.

Mr. Peroni smiled. "I guess your mother has had enough introduction to Barney for today."

"Oh," Lisa said. "I forgot."

"Just don't forget to take good care of that snake. I don't want it getting loose and worrying your mother," Mr. Peroni said.

"Oh, Barney can't get loose," Lisa replied, giving the wire screen a little tap. "He is safe in here."

Barney stopped climbing and looked at Lisa lazily.

The next morning Lisa was up before everyone else. Her mother blinked when she opened the kitchen door. "Where have you been?" she asked, surprised.

"Out in the garage, checking on Barney," Lisa replied, sniffing. "I smell pancakes!"

Mr. Peroni put the newspaper down as Lisa slid into her seat at the table. Mr. Peroni winked at his wife. "First day of vacation and she didn't have to be called to come down. I wonder if we could borrow Barney for the school year."

"Aw, Dad." Lisa grinned. "I just wanted to make sure nothing had bothered him during the night."

Mrs. Peroni looked at Lisa in disbelief. "What would bother a three-foot snake?"

"A big dog, something like that," Lisa replied seriously. "Dad, Mrs. Allen fed Barney yesterday, but he'll need something else in a few days. Could I have three dollars?"

"Whoa now, Lisa." Mr. Peroni shook his head. "You said you were going to take care of Barney yourself. That includes feeding him."

"Well, I guess I could catch some mice," Lisa said thoughtfully.

"Mice? We don't have mice!" Mrs. Peroni set the juice down a little too hard. Lisa wiped the spilled juice with a napkin.

"I know, Mom, but someone must have mice around here."

Mr. Peroni chuckled. "What are you going to do—conduct a house-to-house survey?"

Lisa grinned. "I guess that wouldn't work. But all I need is two. I could raise the rest."

Mrs. Peroni shuddered. "What else do snakes eat?" she asked hastily.

"Birds, squirrels, things like that," Lisa replied. "But Mrs. Allen always fed him white mice, just like the scientists do in laboratories."

Mrs. Peroni hesitated for a moment. Then she said slowly, "I wanted to do some painting and cleaning this summer, and the garage really needs to be cleaned out. I guess Lisa could earn some extra money helping me."

"Thanks, Mom!" Lisa beamed. "You're a lifesaver!"

Mr. Peroni grinned.

"What else could I say?" Mrs. Peroni smiled. "Live mice in the garage? I should hope not!"

Lisa thought her problems were over, but she was wrong. A few weeks later Barney refused to eat his weekly meal.

A Visit to the Vet

Lisa's mother was watching her try to coax Barney to eat when Mr. Peroni drove up after work. "Dad, Barney's sick," Lisa called. "Come and look."

Mr. Peroni closed the car door and walked over to Barney's tank. "Maybe he isn't hungry," he said, tapping the glass. Barney didn't move.

"I don't know. He just doesn't look right," Lisa said.

"Maybe he's getting ready to shed his skin," Mrs. Peroni suggested. "He's certainly grown a lot in a few weeks!"

"If he were shedding his skin, his eyes would be milky," Lisa said. "Look at them. They're as clear as glass."

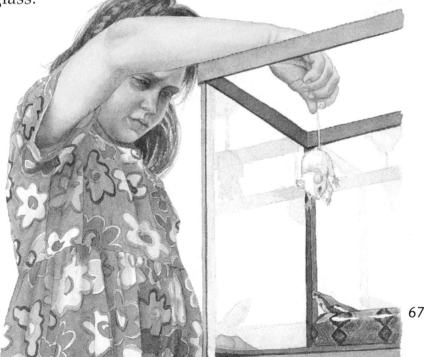

Mrs. Peroni glanced at Lisa's worried face. "Would you feel better if your dad took him to the vet?"

"Oh, yes," Lisa replied.

"Well, let's load his tank into the car," said Mr. Peroni.

Dr. Lee took one look at Barney and knew exactly what was wrong with him. "Your pet has mites under his scales," she told them. "It's not serious now, but without proper care, he could die."

"What can I do?" Lisa asked.

"First of all, clean his tank with ammonia. Then put all of Barney, except his nose, under lukewarm water for ten or fifteen minutes," said the vet. "Most of the mites should drown and fall off."

"Will he be cured after I give him his bath?" Lisa asked.

"He'll need more than one bath to kill all the mites," said the vet. "You must give him two baths a day for the first two days. Then give him one bath a day for a week."

"Then will he be cured?" Lisa asked.

"Not yet," said Dr. Lee. "Wait three or four days for the mites' eggs to hatch, then repeat the treatment. I'll give you a list of the medicines that you will need."

When Lisa and her father got home, they explained Barney's problem to Mrs. Peroni. "In the tub? You want to give the snake a bath in my tub?"

"I'll use my bathroom, Mom," Lisa explained. "And I'll take him right back to the garage. Please, Mom, I don't want him to die."

"Well, all right, but don't you bathe in that tub until that snake is well and the tub is scrubbed clean!"

"Fine, Mom, I don't get too dirty anyway," Lisa said happily.

"That's not what I meant, young lady!" Mom gave a helpless laugh. "You will use our bathroom."

"Aw," Lisa said and left to get Barney. Mrs. Peroni disappeared into the kitchen and didn't come out until Barney was back in the garage.

Each day Lisa washed Barney. When his bath was over, Lisa carried him back to the garage. After the first few days Mrs. Peroni got used to seeing Barney looped over Lisa's arm twice a day. One day Lisa was surprised to see her mom in the doorway watching her bathe Barney.

"Doesn't he try to get loose?" she asked, staring at Barney's head firmly held in Lisa's grasp.

"No, Barney's tame," Lisa said, rubbing Barney's head with her free hand. "He sort of likes it."

Mrs. Peroni watched, fascinated. "How long does that thing actually grow?"

"Probably five or six feet," Lisa answered. "They don't get too big."

"Six feet?" Her mother shuddered. Then she asked with sudden suspicion, "How fast does he grow?"

"Aw, Mom, he's not going to get that long," Lisa replied. "Not this summer, anyway."

"Good!" Mrs. Peroni brightened. She even gave Barney a smile. Barney flickered his tongue as if in response.

"See, Mom," Lisa said. "He likes you."

"Really?" Mrs. Peroni looked at the snake curiously. "I'm not sure I can say the same."

A Surprise at the Meeting

A few days later, Mrs. Peroni had a ladies' meeting at her house. She rushed around all day preparing for the meeting. Around a quarter to four she called Lisa. "Have you given Barney his bath yet?"

"Not yet," she answered. "Why?"

"Why? Because I'm having a meeting at four today. Hurry up and get Barney out of the way!"

"Yes, ma'am!" Lisa hurried to the garage to get Barney. She had Barney wrapped around her shoulders and had just reached the kitchen door when the first car drove up. Lisa hurried inside and raced upstairs to the bathroom.

"Whew!" she said to Barney as she closed the door. "That was close!"

71

Soon Barney was floating happily in lukewarm water, his head safely in Lisa's hand. Lisa stroked his head and talked softly to him. It was after four when Barney was bathed and dried.

"Now how am I going to get you back downstairs?" Lisa asked thoughtfully. "The ladies are all in the living room."

Barney coiled happily around the clothes hamper. "You aren't the easiest thing to hide," Lisa added. Barney rubbed his head against the top of the wicker hamper.

Lisa chuckled. "All right." She opened the top of the hamper. "Get in!"

Barney slithered over the top of the hamper and disappeared into the clothes. Lisa opened the door and peeked over the railing. The room was full of ladies. Lisa sighed and went back to the bathroom. She opened the hamper. Barney was coiled up in the clothes. Lisa closed the lid and sat down. She had to think of a way to get Barney out to the garage.

"I could take the hamper to the garage," she thought. "Barney is asleep, and the hamper doesn't weigh much. Sure, it'll work."

She picked up the hamper and opened the door. Halfway down the stairs, she looked across the room and saw Mrs. Peroni's face. Lisa moved her mouth without actually speaking. "It's Barney."

Mrs. Peroni nodded and stayed where she was. She watched every step Lisa made. She looked like she was holding her breath.

Lisa stepped off the last stair and started across the wooden floor. The hamper wasn't too heavy, but it was more awkward to carry than she had expected. She was doing fine, though, until Mrs. Perkins looked up and saw Mrs. Peroni's face.

"Anna!" she exclaimed. "Whatever is the matter?"

At that moment, Lisa's foot came down on a scatter rug. The rug slipped, and Lisa sprawled on the floor. The hamper slid right into the middle of the room.

"I'll get it! I'll get it!" Lisa yelled as several ladies got up to help.

She was too late.

Three feet of shaken boa constrictor flowed from the overturned hamper and slithered across the floor.

Screams echoed in the room as ladies scrambled in all directions. Lisa dashed after Barney as he disappeared under the couch.

"It's only a boa constrictor," her mother called to the excited ladies.

"Only a boa constrictor!" Mrs. Perkins's voice carried over the noise. "Anna, what are you thinking about, letting your child keep a boa constrictor in the house!"

"It's only a baby," Mrs. Peroni replied rather sharply. "It won't hurt you. Now calm down while I help Lisa."

Most of the ladies gathered on the other side of the room, but a few came to help.

One knelt beside Lisa and her mother. "It doesn't squeeze, does it?"

"No, Barney's tame, and anyway, he's been fed," Lisa replied. "If you just chase him over here, I can catch him."

Mrs. Peroni and some of the other ladies carefully shooed Barney back to Lisa's side of the couch. Lisa picked Barney up and wrapped him around her arm. "There, didn't I tell you he was tame?" Lisa said proudly.

"And he belongs in the garage, not in the house," Mrs. Peroni said firmly. "Out, Lisa!"

As Lisa went out the door, she could hear the ladies' excited comments.

"A boa constrictor! Anna, you're amazing!"

"They're fascinating! Did you know they can swallow an animal larger than their own heads?"

"Yes," Mrs. Peroni replied dryly, "I had noticed."

"But just imagine, keeping one in your house loose like that. Doesn't it make your skin crawl?"

"Well," Lisa heard her mother say hesitantly, "you get used to it after a while. Barney isn't so bad. Why, the other day. . . ."

Lisa grinned and opened the back door. "You hear that, Barney?" She said to the boa constrictor. "You just might not have to stay in the garage all summer after all!"

Just Plain Snake

Nellie Ashe Cooper

People do not always think kindly of boa constrictors. This is probably because of untrue things they have heard about them.

Boa constrictors lie in wait in trees, pounce on people passing by, and swallow them swiftly. The mottled brown and cream coloring of a boa constrictor enables it to hide in trees or on the ground. Heat sensors in the upper lip of the snake help it to detect an animal passing by. The snake lunges swiftly at its prey and constricts it with its coils. The prey, unable to breathe, is dead before it is swallowed.

The boa's prey is not a person or large animal. Like all snakes, boa constrictors have jaw bones that are joined by strong ligaments instead of joints, allowing them to spread far apart so food can be pulled in. This does not mean that they are able to swallow prey of unlimited size. Their usual diet is birds and small mammals like mice and rabbits. They sometimes eat eggs, fish, frogs, toads, lizards, and other snakes. The food is swallowed slowly, and afterward the snake lies motionless for several days while the meal is digested.

Boa constrictors chase people. Boas and other snakes move forward by flexing first one muscle and then another, making waves from head to tail. These waves push against plants, rocks, and other rough surfaces. For climbing, snakes use special muscles to pull the under scales forward and push them back. On the ground or in trees, top speed for a boa is about one mile per hour. At this rate, even a very slow person could outdistance it in no time.

Boa constrictors feel wet and unpleasant. All snakes, including boa constrictors, are covered with dry, overlapping scales on the head and back. Underneath they have larger, overlapping plate scales.

Growth and wear cause the outer layer of a snake's skin to come off from time to time. This *molting* happens more often with young snakes and with snakes living in warmer climates. Before molting, the snake becomes less active, and its eyes have a cloudy look. The snake rubs its head on a rough surface to loosen the old skin. Then it wriggles out, leaving the skin inside out. The new skin that is revealed looks wet because it is shiny and reflects light. It is really quite dry and pleasant to the touch.

Another reason that snakes might be considered unpleasant to touch is that they are sometimes troubled with parasites like mites. They are also troubled with infections that begin when foreign material finds its way between their scales. Both of these cause a buildup of material that smells and feels disgusting. When the problem clears up, the scales are again dry and smooth.

Boa constrictors are not sneaky, speedy, or slimy. They are simply—snaky.

Legends are very old stories. Some might be based on actual happenings; others might have grown out of rumor or gossip. All, however, have changed or grown somewhat in the retelling. The following legend is about William Tell, a brave archer from the country of Switzerland. Long ago, the emperor of Austria claimed Switzerland as his own and sent a man named Gessler to rule the land in his stead. Gessler was a cruel tyrant. One of his greatest pleasures was to see the proud Swiss acknowledge his power. In the marketplace he placed a tall pole. On the top of the pole he placed his hat. Gessler insisted that every Swiss man, woman, or child who passed by the pole should bow to the hat. It is at this point that our story begins.

The Legend of William Tell

illustrated by
Del Thompson

Becky Davis

William Tell strode through the marketplace, his big bow and quiver strapped to his back. Peter almost had to run to keep up with him. Greetings rang out through the marketplace on every side as he and Peter passed. Peter beamed as he heard one man tell a stranger, "That's William Tell, the best archer in the country. Why, one time I saw him split an arrow in flight with another from his quiver. And another time . . ."

Peter looked up at his tall father with pride. He thought about how straight his father held himself—straight as a mountain pine, straight as Gessler's pole.

Peter pulled on his father's sleeve. "Father, the pole is still up there. The one with Gessler's hat on it, I mean."

"Yes, Son, I see it." William Tell smiled down at Peter. "But we will not bow. We must not lose our courage, or we'll never be free again." William Tell began to walk faster. He passed by the large sign attached to the pole without glancing at it. He knew that on the sign Gessler had written in big black letters,

"Whosoever shall not bow to this hat shall thereby take his life into his hands."

The tall man and his son strode on, up the mountain to their home. But in the marketplace their passage had been noted by Gessler's spies. "They did not bow," the spies muttered, hurrying to the palace.

When Gessler heard the spies' story, he ordered, "Bring the great archer—no, wait; bring his son also!"

That same day soldiers appeared at the mountain home of William Tell. When they read the summons to Tell, his face turned pale. "Why should Peter go?"

The soldiers shrugged. "Gessler has ordered it."

Tell strapped on his bow and quiver. He and Peter were escorted down the mountain trail to a meadow where Gessler waited. News of the summons had spread through the town, and the townspeople had gathered in the meadow. They stood silently, watching and listening.

Gessler sneered. "William Tell, I hear many stories about your skill with a bow and arrow. I hear that you can even shoot a hornet out of the air."

William Tell waited without speaking. Peter stood close by his side.

"I also hear that you refuse to bow to my hat!" Gessler's eyes turned to Peter. "You refuse, and your son . . . I hear that you love your only son dearly."

Tell put his hand lightly on Peter's shoulder. "What man would not love his son?" he replied quietly. "Peter is a good, obedient boy."

"I'm sure of that." Gessler's lips curled in a thin smile. "He follows your example well. Perhaps he can help." Gessler's eyes met William Tell's. "I wish to see your skills with a bow and an arrow," he said. "You will shoot an apple from your son's head at one hundred paces! Do it and you go free. Refuse and you both die!"

A murmur arose from the townspeople. A child! Even Gessler could not be that cruel! But the soldiers quickly silenced them. William Tell and his son stood alone before the tyrant.

"You are a wicked man, Gessler," Tell said quietly. "You will soon pay for your wickedness."

Two guards seized Peter, taking him with them as they stepped off the hundred paces. Peter looked back over his shoulder at his father and called, "You can do it, Father!"

The hundred paces were carefully counted; then Peter was turned to face his father. Peter reached for the apple and placed it on his head. He stood straight and tall, just as he had seen his father do so many times.

William Tell drew two arrows from his quiver. The crowd pressed in close behind the soldiers. Then everyone stood still, hardly daring to breathe.

Tell's hand trembled a little as he began to fit one of the arrows into his bow. This was no time for fear. His son's life depended on his skill. Then across the hundred paces, a voice rang out.

"I trust you, Father!"

The great archer lifted his bow. He took careful aim with a steady hand. He let the arrow fly. The arrow pierced the apple and sped beyond the boy.

A great shout rose from the people. Peter came running across the meadow, throwing himself into his father's arms. "I knew you could do it; I knew you could!" he cried.

"Your father was not so sure," said Gessler, snarling. "I see he took two arrows from his quiver when only one was needed!"

William Tell looked over his son's head and spoke in a cold voice. "The second arrow was for thee, tyrant, had I missed my first shot!"

"Seize him!" shrieked the angry ruler.

But the townspeople, who had pressed even closer, threw themselves upon the soldiers. William Tell drew the second arrow and shot Gessler through the heart. In the confusion that followed, he took his boy by the hand and fled. At a nearby lake he found a boat, rowed to the other shore, and escaped with his son into the mountains.

Some people say that when his boy was safe, William Tell returned to lead the Swiss people in their fight for freedom. In any case, the tyrant was dead, and it didn't take long for the brave Swiss people to regain their country and their freedom.

SOMETHING SPECIAL AND SHINY

(from *The Treasure Keeper*)

Anita Williams

illustrated by
Lynn Elam-Jones

Marcos, who lives in Brazil, has many adventures with his sister and his goats; and he collects many treasures. He wants to share his treasures and the happiness they give him with his family on his birthday. Instead, he finds he must use his treasures to help his sister in a very special way.

Part I

No laughing sounded in Marcos's house. No sweet yam or coconut pudding smells drifted from the kitchen. Shades were pulled so that morning sunshine did not come in.

Marcos saw the silent tears washing down Momma's cheeks. Grandmomma was hunched in her chair, head bowed, praying. Poppa didn't go to work. Instead, he tiptoed through the house, looking solemn.

Grandmomma whispered, "Shhh! You must be quiet. Marcia is very sick. We have to walk softly and whisper so she can rest."

Marcos stood behind the door as the doctor came inside. The doctor was short, with a black mustache and a small round belly. He carried a black leather bag, and he wasn't smiling.

The bag was full of strange tubes and bottles and long needles, Marcos imagined.

When the doctor stepped out from Marcia's room, he wore a scowl.

He took Momma to the side and said something in a deep, gravelly voice.

Marcos stared at the wall. Marcia might look crumply and wrinkly, maybe black.

He crept back to his room, making not a speck of noise. Something would make Marcia well, and he had to find it.

His eyes jumped about the room, taking in the green things, yellow things, twisty things, round things, and shiny things.

A breeze stirred the rubber tree's leaves. Mr. Sweet Potato's twisty vines twined down into the clear glass jar. Things alive and things shiny and things fresh—that's what girls liked.

Flowers! Of course, girls liked flowers. Marcia's eyes would smile when she saw a flower dipped in sunshine and wet with morning dew. The golden orchid— Marcia would love it.

Marcos bit his lip, remembering. Grandmomma kept the golden orchid folded in her handkerchief.

And the trouble was, it wasn't gold anymore, but shredded and mostly brown and mostly dry. It was like Marcia—crumply and wilted and broken.

Marcos's eyes rolled, then stopped. There—green as the meadow and shivery as the wet pond stood the little rubber tree, shining. A sick girl needed to look at something alive—and growing and flappy green.

Nobody saw Marcos slip into Marcia's room.

Marcia's soft eyelashes fanned out from closed eyes. A yellow bedspread stretched over her. Her face was pale, but she wasn't black. Hearing him, she squeezed open an eye. Then the other eye flipped open. She saw the rubber tree in its little red tub. Her mouth made a tiny smile. That evening Marcos heard Momma wonder aloud, "Why, where did the beautiful plant come from?"

The very next day Marcos marched right into Marcia's room. He didn't tiptoe either but stepped straight, eyes bright, grinning. Marcia, her face pink and a little pale, smiled back at him.

When she said, "Thank you," in that piping little voice, Marcos laughed. That almost made Marcia giggle. "For the green plant," she murmured.

"It's a sunshiny rubber tree," Marcos told her. "It came from the hot country. It's growing like a giant."

Marcia's smile made Marcos so happy he decided to run to the pond and back. Warm raindrops splashed on his curly head of hair. They slapped at the backs of his legs and patted his shoulders.

He wished Marcia were there, sliding on the slippery grass, laughing and free. The tingly air would waken her and put pink rounds to her cheeks. Whispering breezes might even put a dance in her feet.

Marcos jumped over a knobby log. Marcia wouldn't be able to sing and hop about again unless something happened. Something special and shiny and different had to come to her.

Three big drops, big as tree leaves, slapped his face. Marcos had one idea, two, even three, and maybe four ideas!

Part II

Certainly that girl should have been sleeping when he padded into her room. Twilight hush lay softly. A few chirpy insects were at her window. Two birds kept calling each other.

She opened her eyes, seeing Mr. Sweet Potato, "Oh, that's good," she said.

Every day now Grandmomma laughed as she once did. Momma worked in the kitchen, singing while she stirred and baked. Poppa whistled and went back to work.

Marcos knew what was happening. The green rubber tree and fine Mr. Sweet Potato certainly helped. Now Marcia laughed and could even walk around the room, mostly with a limp.

But more needed to be done. Marcia had to feel so fine she could walk without a limp.

On Wednesday he plunked down the shiny old coin on her bed. "Old and valuable," he told her. Even the coin's nicked edges had been smoothed and polished.

 On Thursday the strange bottle, blue like the sky, green like grass, found itself on Marcia's bed. The sunshine gleamed through its glass diamonds, making them shine like stars.

Marcos's keen eyes whipped around his room. Mr. Beggar Man had the ice rock, and Grandmomma the golden orchid. The only treasure Marcos had left was the ocean in the pink shell.

Mr. Ocean, noisy and crashing and blue, rested in the pink shell with its rippling folds. Marcos put his ear to the pink shell. He could hear the roar and crash of the waves. Mr. Ocean was in there, trying to get out.

That early evening Marcos helped Poppa stack potatoes on the back porch. Momma sat on the steps shelling peas.

"All Marcia needs now is plenty of fresh air," Poppa said.

"True," said Momma, her eyes troubled. "But we're so far from the beach and the water."

Fresh ocean air! Marcia needed it—air sharp and salty, fresh as blue-green water.

At the beach Marcia could hear the slappy water and feel its tingly wetness. Soft damp air would roll in, making her stronger. She would be as pink and sturdy as a sandcastle!

After a while Marcos sat in Marcia's window, letting the outside darkness cool his back. Marcia wore a lacy robe.

"What if," Marcos asked her, "you had the ocean in your room? Think of all the fine fresh air you would get."

"Silly! You can't bring an ocean into a house!" she said, sounding almost like new. "We'd all drown, and besides, we would get wet and cold and fish would eat us up!"

"That might be so," Marcos said, thinking of all the pesty little fish. But the pink shell carried in its ripply folds sunshine and soppy blue air.

He ran to his room, scooped up the pink shell and came rushing, laughing into her room.

"Here! Just listen!"

Marcia examined the glorious little shell. Its outsides were white; its insides wriggly pink. She held it to her right ear, face glowing. She held it to her left ear, smiling. The funny noisy ocean roared as if it were angry, then crashed as if it were glad.

The waves started from far away, rolling, rushing, crashing hard on the sandy beach. They swept in, bringing wetness and freshness and green seaweed. Marcos and his sister listened, bouncing up and down with their laughing.

Mr. Ocean was there, in Marcia's room!

And Marcia was getting stronger every minute.

A New Land

The Diary of George Shannon

Eileen M. Berry / illustrated by Del Thompson

In 1803, President Thomas Jefferson sent an expedition, the Corps of Discovery, to explore the Louisiana Territory. Meriwether Lewis and William Clark, leaders of the expedition, hoped to find a water route to the west coast, develop a system of trade with the Native Americans, and study the land.

George Shannon was a member of the Corps of Discovery. Although this account is fictional, the events it describes actually occurred, and all of the characters are real.

Along the Missouri

May 13, 1804—

Tomorrow we set sail. I'm glad the winter of training is over, and we can finally get on with our adventure. Clark seems eager to be off. We'll all fit nicely in three pirogues to ride the river. There are nine of us from the Kentucky backwoods, and I'm the youngest of the group. We also have two hired French boatmen, Clark's slave York, several squads of soldiers, and Clark's dog Seaman. George Drouillard, whom we call "Drewyer," has gone on ahead and will meet us with Lewis at St. Charles. He's an expert in Plains Indian sign language, and he will be our interpreter on this expedition.

May 26, 1804—

We passed La Charette today—the last white settlement on the Missouri. We're sailing against a swift current, so the going is slow. Nothing ahead but wilderness.

August 2, 1804—

We had a council with Missouri and Oto chiefs today. Lewis tried to make it clear that we come peacefully as friends and want them on our side. We gave them blankets and peace medals, and Lewis fired a few rounds from an air gun. They seemed impressed with that. President Jefferson wants us to make friends with the Indian nations as much as possible. I think he would have been pleased with today's council.

Mandan chief

Meeting with chiefs

Lewis with air gun

Peace medal

September 11, 1804—

I am relieved to be back with the men again.
I got separated from Drewyer while we were hunting,
and I lost my bearings. I've been trying to catch up
with the rest of the party for more than two weeks.
I ran out of bullets to hunt with, and I nearly starved.
I told Lewis I would gladly eat even some of his
"portable soup" right now. But when I saw the thick,
gooey stuff, I changed my mind.

October 3, 1804—

We saw some more of those interesting little
creatures on the prairie today. They seem to be a type
of squirrel but they bark like a dog. I heard one of the
men calling them prairie dogs, and I think the name
will stick. We've also seen huge herds of buffalo on
the plains. Clark estimated that we saw about three
thousand buffalo today. We've also seen some
unusual birds with green and black feathers. Pretty
little things. I believe they're called magpies.

Buffalo Prairie dogs Magpie

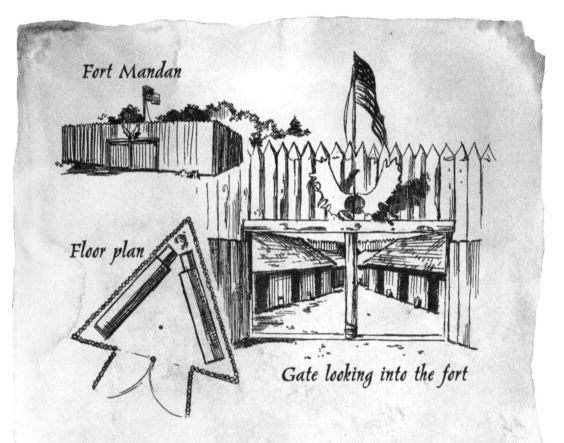

Fort Mandan

Floor plan

Gate looking into the fort

November 3, 1804—

We've reached the place where we'll spend the winter. Our neighbors will be the Mandan and Hidatsa. We got a start building Fort Mandan today. It is roughly triangular in shape. Each of the three walls will be fifty-six feet long. Within the fort we'll build eight log cabins arranged in a *V*. We'll have a shed for storing our supplies with a flat roof for a sentry to stand on. We should be cozy and safe for the winter. It's certainly better than living in tents.

December 25, 1804—

This is definitely the strangest Christmas I have ever spent. Ma and Pa would have been shocked to see our Christmas guests at Fort Mandan—the Indians. We had some lively fiddle music around a fire, and the laughter made us forget about the cold for a while. But I did feel a little homesick when I thought of Ma's Christmas turkey.

January 23, 1805—

We've been joined by another French Canadian— Toussaint Charbonneau. His wife Sacajawea is a Shoshone—not much more than a girl, but seems older. She is quiet and a hard worker. She's expecting a child soon.

February 11, 1805—

Sacajawea's baby, Jean Baptiste, was born today. We all feel kind of like uncles. It's funny to see all of us making such a fuss over a baby. But I have to say he is a cute little thing. He's small but seems hardy enough. I hope he makes it. We all have a little trouble pronouncing his French name. Clark has decided to call him "Pomp." We're glad to have him with us.

Baby Pomp

Through Uncharted Lands

April 7, 1805—

We're off again! All the men were in high spirits as we set sail today. Up to this point, we've had maps to guide us, but from now on the territory is truly uncharted. Charbonneau and Sacajawea have agreed to accompany us. We are counting on Sacajawea's help and interpreting skills as we travel through Shoshone country. Jean Baptiste seems quite comfortable strapped to his mother's back, and the rocking of the boat often lulls him right off to sleep. Other new members of our party are a prairie dog and four magpies.

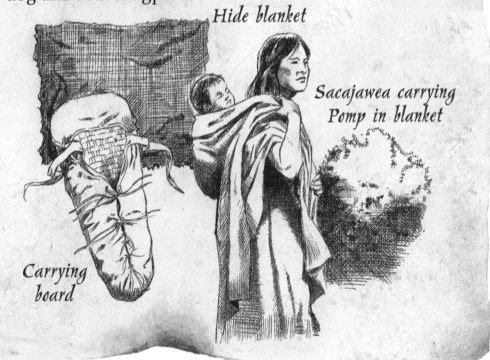

Hide blanket

Sacajawea carrying Pomp in blanket

Carrying board

Pawprint

Grizzly bear

May 14, 1805—

We had two close calls today. When we spotted a grizzly bear, six of us went ashore after it. The bear saw us and charged. I can never forget how fierce the bear looked as it ran straight at us. We fired a round of bullets at the bear, and it took several hits but seemed not even to feel them. It just kept coming. After shooting a second round without slowing the bear down, we turned and ran for our lives. I made it to our canoe, but four others reloaded and fired another round at the bear. They ended up jumping off an embankment with the bear right on their heels. Finally someone fired a shot through its brain and killed it. We dragged the carcass to shore and found eight bullets inside it!

Later, one of our boats almost sank. Wind struck it, whipped it out of control, and flung it on its side. Cruzatte, our boatman, managed to get the pirogue to shore with Sacajawea sitting in the bow, bailing water and catching our things as they floated past. Nothing of value was lost. What a day! We will all sleep well tonight, I'm certain of that.

June 15, 1805—

We've been passing through a region of strange rock formations that the French call *the Badlands*. The Missouri has divided into two forks, and we've had some disagreement among ourselves as to which fork was the true Missouri. While trying to decide which fork to take, Lewis discovered a great waterfall partway up the southwest fork today. That convinced us that fork was the Missouri. Lewis called the falls the grandest sight he has ever seen. We'll have to take the pirogues ashore to get around them. This will be no small haul—I'd say at least twenty miles, maybe more.

The Badlands

The Great Falls

August 12, 1805—

Today we crossed a ridge of the Rocky Mountains. I've never seen anything like these mountains— so grand and glorious. We had a drink from a clear mountain stream. The view from the top of the ridge was spectacular. There are many more mountains ahead to cross, but we feel we've reached a milestone. Each step brings us closer to the Pacific.

August 17, 1805—

We've come into the territory of the Shoshone people, and today we found out that the Shoshone chief, Cameahwait, is Sacajawea's brother. The two haven't seen each other for years. For the first time on this expedition, I saw Sacajawea cry. She tried her best to interpret for her brother, but she kept breaking down into tears of joy.

Shoshone chief in ceremonial dress

Thatched teepee

Shoshone baskets

Sacajawea meets her brother

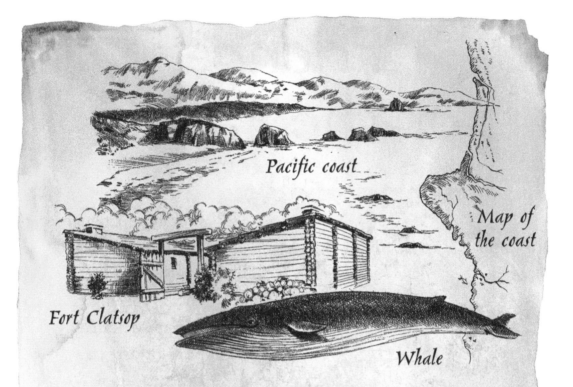

Pacific coast

Map of the coast

Fort Clatsop

Whale

November 10, 1805—

What a sight! After more than a year, we've come to the end of the trail, and the great Pacific Ocean spreads out before us as far as the eye can see. We had a jolly time in the camp tonight. Some of the men boiled a little salt from sea water, and we enjoyed salt on our meat for the first time in months. Sacajawea insists on seeing a whale, so we will take her on a whale hunt tomorrow. We'll build another fort and winter here; then we'll head back the way we've come. I can hardly wait to see my family again. What stories I'll have to tell.

Friends of the Prairie

Eileen M. Berry

If you visit the plains of such states as Kansas, South Dakota, and Wyoming, you may notice piles of dirt in the middle of nowhere. Watch carefully. Stay very quiet. You just might see a furry brown head pop out of a dirt pile. Wait a few seconds, and the animal will stand to its full height—about twelve inches— and look around.

The western plains are the most likely places
to discover prairie dog *towns*. These towns look
like many mounds of dirt with craters in the tops.
Each mound is the entrance to a prairie dog burrow.
Each town is home to a whole colony of prairie dogs.

Prairie dogs are not really dogs at all. They are
small animals closely related to chipmunks and
squirrels. But they do live on the prairie, and explorers
called them *dogs* because they make barking sounds.
Over the years, the name has seemed like a good one
to keep.

Most prairie dogs are brown with white bellies. They can be as long as fifteen inches and weigh up to three pounds. Like squirrels, they have short ears, flat heads, and stubby legs. Their short, thin tails are tipped with white or black. God has given them long claws for digging their burrows and strong teeth for cutting and grinding their food.

Prairie dogs' favorite food is grass. The prairies provide many different types of grass for them to try. Sometimes they stand on all four legs to graze, but most sit up, hold their grass stems in their paws, and look around while they eat.

Prairie dogs are sociable creatures. They seem to enjoy playing together, digging together, eating together, or sometimes just sitting with their paws around each other.

But prairie dogs do not always act friendly toward one another. Within each town are smaller groups or "clans" with carefully guarded boundaries. If a prairie dog from another clan tries to cross those boundaries, fierce fights can break out. Members of a prairie dog clan greet each other by touching noses or mouths in a "kiss" of recognition.

Prairie dog towns are not very quiet places. Barks ring out often for many different reasons. Prairie dogs bark when they are defending their territory, protecting their young, or arguing over their food. One special, high-pitched bark is different from the others. It is a warning of danger.

Prairie dogs have many enemies. Warning barks could mean danger from above, where eagles and hawks circle and swoop. Or a warning bark could mean danger from below, where snakes slither without a sound and ferrets creep through the tall grasses. At the sound of the warning barks, prairie dogs spring into action. If they have time, they dart into their burrows. If they are too far from a burrow to hide, they flatten themselves against the ground where they may not be noticed.

Prairie dogs' burrows are their most important form of protection. When in danger, they will sometimes stay inside their burrows for an hour at a time. Burrows are made up of several underground "rooms" connected by tunnels. Prairie dogs wait and listen for the danger to pass. Then one or two of the braver ones will poke their heads out, look around, and sound the "all-clear" bark to let the others know that the world is safe again.

Recently, scientists have learned that prairie dogs help the land in several ways. They are constantly churning up dirt, giving the soil beneath the earth's surface a chance to air out and be fertilized. The holes they dig allow water to reach deeper layers of soil. The soil they bring to the  surface is broken down into food for plants. In spite of their small size, these animals are one of the prairie's greatest friends.

Toys from Nature

Steffi Adams

illustrated by Stephanie True and Janet Davis

Imagine for a moment that you are all alone in a meadow on a beautiful day in early summer. The birds are singing. The daisies and clover are swaying in the gentle breeze.

Now pretend that you must spend the whole day in this meadow. You do not have any toys. How will you spend the day? What will you do? Will you miss your friends, books, and toys?

Pioneer children did not always have a hard time filling their days. They often worked from sunrise to sunset with their parents.

But when these children had some free time, they often played in the woods and meadows, making many of their own games and toys. With a little work and imagination, they turned ordinary objects of nature into treasured playthings.

The children often built playhouses by piling pine needles into the rough shapes of chests, tables, and beds. When their make-believe houses were finished, the girls pretended to cook, sew, and care for their special dolls that they made from grass and twigs. Apples, pears, turnips, potatoes, nuts, and even daisies sometimes made special dolls' heads. After using corncobs and cornstalks to make other dolls, the girls would twist corn silk into yellow braids for dolls' hair.

The dolls were not finished until the girls had dressed them. In the girls' hands, dried cornhusks tied with corn silk became lovely dresses. Leaves of all shapes and sizes became aprons, hats, and sunshades. Tiny daisy chains and seed necklaces completed the dolls' outfits.

When the dolls were dressed, the girls built dollhouses. Sometimes they made "log cabins" with corncobs. At other times they just cleared the dirt away from big tree roots to form "dugouts."

Of course, each dollhouse needed furniture. By sticking burrs together, the girls made tables, chairs, and beds. They built cradles from cornhusks and milkweed pods. Tiny pine needles made perfect brooms. The girls even made acorn bowls, rose-hip teacups, and birch-bark drinking cups.

The dolls' tables looked bare without food, so the girls gathered berries and seeds. Pulling off daisy petals, the girls used the flowers' centers as "pumpkin pies." Then they made thick mud pies and weak mud tea.

Pioneer boys also played with objects from the meadows and woods. They played games and built toys that improved their skills in fishing, hunting, tracking, and fighting.

Some of these toys were simple to make. By tying a vine to a tree branch or a cane stalk, the boys had a fishing pole. In their eyes, a large stick became a snorting horse.

The boys often used simple toys to improve their aim. They made flat stones skip and slide over the surface of rivers and streams. Hard, round berries served as marbles. Pointing certain flowers, like the touch-me-nots, at targets, the boys popped the seeds. They threw darts made from half a corncob and four chicken feathers, and they carried long cornstalk "spears" as they followed wild animal tracks on their stick horses.

Other games and toys were harder to make. Using their pocketknives, the boys hollowed out elder and willow branches to make bean shooters or blowpipes.

The boys also made noisemakers with their knives. From dandelion stems they formed horns, and from weeping willow branches they cut willow whistles. They also carved flat wooden paddles, called "bull-roarers." When the boys tied these bull-roarers to strings and swung them around and around, the flat paddles sounded like angry, snorting bulls.

Down by the stream the boys built twig-and-leaf "flutter mills" that turned like windmills as the flowing water lifted each leaf.

Pioneer boys and girls played with all of these games and toys—and many more. They filled their playtimes with activity because their imaginations never stopped working.

Just suppose that you are still alone in a meadow. Now how would you spend the day? Could you think of more things to do?

The Secret Pony

Unattributed
illustrated by Kathy Pflug

The Stahl family left their home in Germany in 1741 and sailed for America. They purchased land outside Philadelphia and began to build a farm. Within the year a sturdy house and barn stood on the land. Then the family turned their attention to building fences and farming. For the youngest son, the fences couldn't be built fast enough.

A Lost Pony

The sun was shining and the birds were singing, but ten-year-old Jacob Stahl hardly noticed the beauty around him. It was market day, and his brothers, Ernst and Hans, were loading the wagon. They chattered as he herded the family's cows from the huge red barn.

"Nothing ever happens to me," Jacob said to himself as the last cow left the barn. "Milk the cows. Take them to pasture. Bring them home before supper. Milk them again—my days never change."

Jacob grumbled all the way to the pasture. The herd of cows spread out across the green grass, the bells around their necks clanging as they lowered their noses and began grazing. Jacob plopped down into the sweet-smelling clover.

"I can't wait until the fences are done," he said to the cows. "Then you will be put in the pasture, and I can do something besides sit here all day."

Jacob forgot about the bull-roarer he had made yesterday and the flutter mill that still whirled down in the stream. He forgot about the cave he had found and kept for his secret place. All he could think about was that he couldn't go to the market with his brothers.

Suddenly Jacob sat up. A tiny, reddish brown pony with a coal black mane and tail was galloping toward him!

Jacob whistled. "She's beautiful!" he said out loud.

At the sound of Jacob's whistle, the pony stopped in her tracks and stared at the boy. Then she arched her neck, shook her head, and galloped off.

Jacob held his breath while the pony swerved in and out among the cows. The cows just flicked their tails and kept eating.

"Where did she come from?" Jacob wondered. The pony lay down and rolled over and over in the soft grass.

Each time Jacob tried to get near the pony, she snorted, laid her ears back, and galloped away. At last Jacob sat quietly and watched her graze beside the cows.

"I'll catch you on the morrow," he said. "Won't everyone be surprised when I come home leading a pony!"

The next morning Jacob was dressed five minutes before his mother called him. He beat Ernst downstairs and helped Hans milk the cows. Then he gobbled down his breakfast.

"Why are you in such a hurry?" asked his father in German.

"It's spring!" said Jacob. He drank the last drop of creamy milk, leaving a white mustache on his upper lip.

"I want to go to the pasture with Jacob," said nine-year-old Abigail.

Jacob sighed with relief when his mother shook her head.

"We must clean the house," Frau Stahl reminded her daughter. She turned to Jacob and added, "Wipe your mouth, Son."

Jacob rubbed the back of his hand across his mouth. He grabbed a hunk of bread, some cheese, and an apple. Then he put on his hat and ran to the barn.

As he walked behind the cows a few minutes later, Jacob thought of just the right name for the pony.

"Molasses!" said Jacob, thinking of his mother's thick, reddish brown molasses. "That's what I'll call her—Molasses!"

Jacob made sure that the cows were settled into the lower pasture before he searched for the pony. He held the apple in his left hand and dangled a rope from his other hand.

"Molasses! Oh, Molasses! Where are you?" he called.

A soft whinny came from across the creek.

Jacob hummed as he walked very slowly toward the creek. He stopped at the edge of the water and held out the apple.

"Come on, girl. Here's your breakfast," said Jacob.

Molasses sniffed the apple and then opened her mouth. Carefully Jacob moved his right hand toward the pony's shoulder.

"Come a little closer, Molasses," he said.

The pony took a few steps forward and snatched the apple from Jacob's hand. While she chewed, Jacob rubbed her forehead and patted her neck.

"That's a good girl," he said. He was still patting Molasses when he noticed the brand on her left side.

"Who is *IW?*" he wondered. "I don't know anyone with those initials."

Molasses just nuzzled Jacob's face.

"Well, I'll find out who you belong to later," Jacob decided as he slipped the rope over the pony's head. "Let's get out of this creek."

Molasses snorted and shook her head. She pulled hard against the rope as she backed into the water.

"Now, don't be stubborn," said Jacob. He followed the pony into the creek.

Jacob braced himself and pulled with all his might. Without warning, Molasses gave up. Jacob tumbled into the water. Molasses grabbed Jacob's hat in her teeth and galloped away.

Jacob's Secret

That night Jacob still didn't tell his family about the pony. He thought about looking in the newspaper his father had brought home from the market. Perhaps there was something about a missing pony. Jacob picked up the paper and then put it down without reading it.

"I wish Molasses *could* be mine," he thought to himself. Somehow, after he had named the pony, it seemed more like his own.

The next morning, as soon as the cows were munching the thick green grass, Jacob searched for the pony. He found her near his secret cave. It was then the thought came to him.

"Maybe I wouldn't have to give you up right away," he said, peering into the cave. "This is the perfect hiding place. Molasses, you can be my secret for a little while!"

All afternoon, as the cows grazed nearby, Jacob piled rocks and tree branches in front of the cave. He left a gap just wide enough for Molasses to walk in and out of her "home."

"When I cover this hole with a small bush, you'll be safe," said Jacob as he tied the pony inside the cave. "Nothing can hurt you in here."

Molasses pricked up her ears at the sound of Jacob's voice and then rested her head on his shoulder. "This is a fine home," she seemed to say.

As the days passed, Jacob and Molasses became good friends. As soon as the cows were in the pasture, Jacob ran to untie Molasses.

Molasses always felt frisky after spending the night in the dark cave. When Jacob turned her loose outside, she charged toward him, not stopping until the last second.

When Jacob called, she pricked up her ears and galloped to him. She especially loved to sniff out the carrots and apples Jacob saved for her.

Sometimes when Jacob was sitting on her back, she would suddenly make a right-hand turn. Each time she pulled this trick, Jacob sailed straight through the air and landed with a "thud" on the hard earth.

"You know that trick too well," Jacob groaned, picking himself up for the umpteenth time. Then he thought guiltily, "I wonder how many times you tried that on your real owner?" Jacob pushed the thought out of his mind as he and Molasses followed the cows.

Jacob never stayed angry with Molasses, not even when she plopped down in the creek just after he had brushed her with an old comb.

As the days grew warmer, Molasses often stretched out in the pasture. When Jacob first saw the pony lying on her right side with her eyes closed, he thought she was dead. Then he saw the "dead" pony swat a fly with her tail.

"Don't frighten me like that," Jacob scolded.

Molasses just lifted her head and seemed to say, "Why don't you join me?"

"I can't keep Molasses hidden forever," Jacob thought. "Soon I'll have to tell my father. Then he will look for the owner."

Even though he didn't want to lose Molasses, Jacob worried about Molasses's owner. How old was he? Was he searching for his pony?

The Decision

One day, Jacob thought of a plan that might help him keep the pony.

"Molasses may not have an owner anymore," he said to himself. "I will read the advertisements in the newspaper. If no one places an advertisement for my pony, maybe Father will let me keep her."

A few days later Jacob eagerly waited for his father to return from the market in Philadelphia.

"Did you bring the *Gazette?*" he asked as soon as his father stepped down from the wagon.

"It's in the back," Herr Stahl replied. "I thought you didn't like to practice your English."

"I'm getting better every week," said Jacob. "I can understand most of the words."

"Well, help me unload the wagon," said his father. "You can read the newspaper after our Bible study."

As soon as the Bible study was over, Jacob reached for the newspaper. Quickly he turned to the advertisements. There was nothing about Molasses!

Each week when his father brought the paper home from the market, Jacob was the first to ask for it.

Sometimes there was an advertisement for a lost horse. Jacob always held his breath until he was sure that the advertisement had been written about some horse other than Molasses.

Then one day Jacob's hopes were shattered. His heart seemed to stop as he read the following words:

17 June 1742: Strayed, about two months ago, from the Northern Liberties of this city, a small bay mare branded IW. . . . She, being but little and bare-footed, cannot be supposed to have gone far; therefore, if any of the town boys find her and bring her to the subscriber, they shall, for their trouble, have liberty to ride her when they please. William Franklin.

Jacob gasped when he read the name of Molasses's owner. William Franklin was Benjamin Franklin's eleven-year-old son!

Slowly Jacob put the paper down on the table. His father looked up. "Why, Jacob," he said, "what is the matter?"

"Molasses," he choked and ran outside.

Herr Stahl found Jacob sitting on the steps, crying. He sat down beside the boy and waited. At last Jacob raised his head.

"The pony in the advertisement is Molasses," he said.

"Molasses?" asked his father.

"Yes," replied Jacob. "I found a pony and hid her in a cave."

For a moment Herr Stahl didn't speak. Then he said quietly, "You had better tell me all of it."

Jacob told his story haltingly, trying not to think of Molasses waiting by the creek, Molasses running in the sunshine, Molasses tucked safely into the secret cave.

When Jacob finished, Herr Stahl shook his head sadly. "You have done wrong, Son," he said. "The pony was not yours to keep."

Jacob hung his head. "I know," he replied. "I'm sorry, Father. I wanted her so badly . . ." He looked at his father. "I want to return her myself, Father."

Herr Stahl nodded. "Yes. Next market day, we will take the pony to Mr. Franklin. In the meantime, bring the pony up to the barn. You must take good care of her."

"Yes, sir." Jacob started to get up.

His father spoke again. "Jacob, your job is to take care of the cows. You will not be allowed to play with the pony again, only take care of her."

"I understand, Father." Jacob walked away slowly.

On the next market day the Stahls' wagon jolted down the narrow, bumpy road into Philadelphia. Molasses trotted happily at the end of her rope, but Jacob did not smile at the sight of her tossing head.

"What will Mr. Franklin say to me?" he wondered.

When the wagon stopped in front of the house and shop on Market Street, Molasses pawed the ground. She was glad to be home.

"I'll wait for you here," said Herr Stahl as Jacob climbed down from the wagon.

At that moment the shop door opened, and a large man with a cheerful face stepped outside.

Jacob swallowed. "Mr. Franklin," he called. The man turned around. "I found your son's pony, sir," he stammered.

Ben Franklin followed him to the back of the wagon. "Well, so you have," he said, patting the pony. "It is Lady Anne! You've taken good care of her. I will keep my promise. You may ride her whenever you come to town."

Jacob looked at Molasses longingly. Then he shook his head. "I'm sorry, sir. I hid your son's pony because I wanted to keep her. I don't deserve a reward."

Mr. Franklin looked at Jacob kindly. "I won't try to change your mind, but I do understand how much a boy can want a pony. William's not much older than you are. He'll be glad to get Lady Anne back."

Jacob swallowed and nodded. He turned to climb back into the wagon.

"Jacob," called Mr. Franklin, "stop in to see William next market day. I won't try to change your mind, but William might!"

Herr Stahl waved to Mr. Franklin and clucked to the horses. The wagon lurched forward as Mr. Franklin led Molasses around the corner of the printing shop. Jacob turned to his father.

"Do you think," he began hesitantly, then stopped.

His father gave Jacob a thoughtful look. "You know, Jacob," he said, "Mr. Franklin was right. You did take good care of Molasses. And you take good care of the cows. You took care of them even when you were playing with Molasses."

Jacob looked puzzled. "That was my job, Father."

"And sometimes you didn't like your job."

"Sometimes," Jacob replied. "I guess I got tired of the same thing every day."

"But you still did your job well," Herr Stahl said. "And I think you have learned not to keep someone else's property, haven't you?"

"Yes, sir."

"The fences are up, and next week we will put the cows into the fenced pasture. We will find something else for you to do, Jacob." Herr Stahl smiled at Jacob. "And from now on, you go to market with the other boys. Would you like that?"

"Yes, sir!" Jacob replied happily. A new job and market day! And maybe someday . . . maybe he could visit, just visit, William and Molasses.

News About Ads

Wendy M. Harris

1704

Since colonial days, newspapers have been important to the United States. These papers were very plain and had few pictures. Often much of the paper was covered with ads for buying and selling all kinds of goods and for job openings. Papers also listed ads of people who offered services, like giving music lessons.

1892

Notice the changes in the second paper. It was printed over a hundred years later. By then, newspapers looked different. They had more columns, sketches, drawings, and cartoons.

1999

Newspapers today have still more changes! This paper was printed in the late 1900s. One of the biggest changes in the looks of the newspaper is photographs. Even color photographs are now possible.

142

One thing that hasn't changed in newspapers is advertising by individuals to buy and sell goods. Today these ads are called *classified* ads and are found in the classified section of the newspaper.

Large newspapers have indexes telling the location of different parts of the paper. If your newspaper does not have an index, you can usually find classified ads in the back pages.

To place a classified ad, the advertiser calls the newspaper office. A worker takes down the information, tells how much the ad will cost, and sends the person a bill. The cost of the ad is based on how many words it has. The advertiser mails a check to the newspaper office to pay for the ad.

Clothing

BELL BOTTOMS, bright yellow. Worn once. Will never wear again. $5. Call 210-9878.

FUR COAT, soft, brown, perfect for dinner parties, $20 or BO. x1211

ORANGE RAINCOAT, Famous designer Attilio, $115. 420-6792

PLATFORM SHOES, Alligator skin, very high. $45 firm. 232-4589

Office Equip.

BIG BROWN DESK, Oak, $150 or BO. 320-1112

CHAIR, gray and black, swivels nicely. 230-4002

FAX MACHINE, Missing top cover. $85. 423-5436

COMPUTER MOUSE, works fine. Needs a computer to give it a home! $110. Call 220-6899

Pets

CAT, big and orange, found at the park, free to good home. 345-0987

FERRET, very friendly, good with kids, $2. 151-8524

MAGGIE, pet hamster, good for schools, $56. Call 223-9000.

TOUCAN, likes to eat cereal and go on vacations, very easy to care for. FREE. 275-7986.

Classified ads are listed in groups. All ads of the same kind are printed together under a title. Look at the sample groups of ads. These groups make it easier to find only the ads you are interested in.

Each ad tells what is being offered and gives a little information about that item. The ad also lists a price. Last, a telephone number is listed. Anyone interested in that item can call the person who placed the ad for more information.

Classified ads have been around for a long time and are useful to us and to newspaper companies. The ads help people find jobs and buy things they want. The ads help the newspaper company too. The money people pay to place ads is used to help pay for the cost of the newspapers. Without this money, a higher price would have to be charged for the papers.

Phillis Wheatley:
Slave Girl of Old Boston

Steffi Adams

illustrated by Del Thompson and Johanna Berg

In the summer of 1761 Susannah Wheatley was looking for a new slave to train to be her companion. On the slave block of Boston she found a small, seven-year-old girl. The child was dressed only in the tattered remnants of a carpet. She was sick too, possibly as a result of the long ocean voyage on the slave ship. Other slave buyers passed her over because of her condition, but Mrs. Wheatley saw something she liked in the child's face. Having paid the slaver's price, she took the child to the Wheatley home on King Street and put her to bed.

A Place to Begin

The Wheatley twins entered the sickroom quietly. Eighteen-year-old Mary pulled up a chair next to the bed. Nathaniel stood beside a bedpost and looked over at his mother, who sat on the other side of the bed.

145

"How is she?" he whispered.

"She is better," Mrs. Wheatley replied, "although she coughs often. It will take her a while to get her strength back, even with medicine."

"She's a pretty little thing," Mary said, looking at the dark face against the pillow. "What are you going to call her?"

"Phillis," Mrs. Wheatley replied. "Phillis Wheatley. It's a good name, and it suits her. Let's let her rest now."

As the days went by, the rest and the medicine did their work. Phillis grew stronger every day. When she was up and about, she found that she was the youngest member of the Wheatley household. Phillis responded to the family's kindness with affection. Mrs. Wheatley, surprised at how quickly Phillis learned to speak English, asked Mary to become Phillis's teacher. Mary gave Phillis reading lessons, and in sixteen months Phillis was reading difficult passages in the Bible.

One day Mrs. Wheatley found Phillis trying to write on the wall with a piece of charcoal.

"Has Mary taught you to write?" Mrs. Wheatley asked in astonishment.

"No, ma'am," Phillis answered. "When I think of words that I have read in the Bible, I want to write them down so I won't forget them."

"We'll have to teach you to write," said the amazed Mrs. Wheatley. "Mary will get you some paper and a pen."

Phillis did learn to write and went on to study Latin and the classics when she was twelve. She loved poetry and liked to write her own poems.

"Someday I would like to write poems like this one," she told Mrs. Wheatley, showing her a favorite poem in a book of poetry.

"I wouldn't be surprised if you do, Phillis," her mistress replied, shaking her head in amusement. "You do amaze me, child."

Realizing that Phillis had special abilities, the Wheatleys required only light housework from her, allowing her to continue her studies.

During the year that Phillis turned twelve the Stamp Act was repealed. The repeal of the tax that had been so despised by many of the colonists was a reason for rejoicing and celebrating.

Phillis could scarcely control her excitement. Running from window to window, she watched the colored ribbons fluttering in the branches of the trees.

"They're beautiful!" she exclaimed, turning to Mrs. Wheatley. "When do the fireworks begin?"

"You'll have to wait until nightfall," Mrs. Wheatley said, smiling at the eager girl. "Run and help Mary put candles in all the windows. Tonight we'll celebrate the repeal of the Stamp Act."

Phillis hurried to obey. By the time she and Mary had finished, it was getting dark outside. "It's time we left," Mr. Wheatley said. "There will be a crowd on Boston Common tonight."

The family and Phillis rode in the Wheatley carriage to Boston Common. They joined the crowd and waited for the fireworks to begin. Phillis gasped in delight when rockets shot into the sky and pinwheels scattered sparks in every direction on the ground.

"It's wonderful," she said to her mistress. "I'll write a poem to tell King George so!"

When she got home, Phillis lit a candle and picked up her quill pen. She wrote a poem thanking King George for repealing the Stamp Act. Mrs. Wheatley was pleased with the poem and encouraged Phillis to write more. Phillis liked to write about events that happened in the city or at home.

One day she heard two visitors at the Wheatley home talking about a narrow escape from an accident at sea.

"Where would those men have gone if they had died? To heaven or to hell?" she wondered.

Picking up her pen, she began to write about the two men. In her poem she wrote about heaven and hell. On December 21, 1767, a Rhode Island newspaper printed the finished poem. Phillis was thirteen years old.

A Place to Stay

Looking about Boston, Phillis saw many changes taking place. She wrote more poems as British soldiers marched through the city. She wrote while the citizens and the soldiers shouted insults at each other. She wrote when everywhere people talked of war.

In August a British preacher named George Whitefield arrived in Boston. Phillis attended the services with the other slaves and listened carefully. She liked what she heard and looked forward to other meetings. But on Sunday morning in late September, a man rode up King Street shouting, "Whitefield is dead! Whitefield is dead!"

The thought of death shocked Phillis. "Mr. Whitefield is in heaven, but where will I be when I die?" she thought. "He showed me the way of salvation. I must follow."

Phillis wrote a poem describing her sorrow over Mr. Whitefield's death. Many colonial newspapers printed the poem, and it was even published in London, England.

The important men of Boston were amazed. "This girl has been in our land for only nine years," they said. "She could not write this!"

Many of them came to the Wheatley home to speak to Phillis. Only when they talked to her did they believe that she had actually written the poem.

On August 18, 1771, Phillis was baptized in the Old South Church. "Ten years ago I saw my mother pour out offerings to the sun," she said. "God's mercy has brought me from those heathen practices to His salvation."

Phillis wrote many more poems, often staying up late into the night. She began to get sick again; so the Wheatleys sent her into the country, hoping the fresh air would help. But Phillis only grew worse.

Finally the doctor suggested a sea voyage. "Perhaps salt air will make her feel better," he said.

Mrs. Wheatley nodded. "Nathaniel has to go to London on business. Phillis can go with him to prepare her poems for publication in London. The countess of Huntingdon has agreed to be her patron."

So Phillis found herself skimming across the ocean in a passenger ship. In London she had the pleasure of being presented to nobility. She also saw her first volume of poetry go to the printer. But one day a letter came from America. Mrs. Wheatley was very ill. Phillis set sail for America in July.

When Phillis arrived in Boston, Mary took her quickly to Mrs. Wheatley's bedside.

"How are you feeling?" Phillis asked quietly.

Mrs. Wheatley struggled to sit up. "I feel a little better each day," she said. "I'm just glad to have you home, Phillis."

But Mrs. Wheatley did not get better. She grew weaker and weaker. Mary and Phillis stayed by her side.

One month after Phillis had arrived home, Mr. Wheatley called her into his study.

"Phillis," Mr. Wheatley said, "are you happy with us, truly happy?"

"Why, of course," Phillis replied. "Why do you ask?"

"Your English friends think that you should be set free," he answered. "Would you like your freedom, Phillis?"

"I believe that God has planted the love of freedom in every person," Phillis said slowly. "God has released my soul from the bondage of sin. If He wishes, He will release my body in His own way and time. Until that day comes, I will obey you as my master because it pleases God."

"God has answered your prayers," said Mr. Wheatley. "I will have the paper prepared. You will have your freedom."

"Thank you, Mr. Wheatley!" Phillis cried, tears running down her cheeks. "God bless you!"

"Phillis, you have become one of the family." Mr. Wheatley shook his head sadly. "Where will you go now?"

Phillis thought for a moment. Freedom meant that she would have her own lodgings. The money from the sale of her books would be her chief source of income, allowing her time to write another volume for publication. She would be on her own!

But upstairs, the woman who had accepted her as a child lay ill, perhaps dying. Phillis turned to Mr. Wheatley. "That can wait," she said. "May I stay and care for my mistress?"

"Of course, Phillis." Mr. Wheatley smiled. "Of course you may stay. Mrs. Wheatley would be heartbroken to lose you now. She loves you."

"And I love her," Phillis replied.

"Then let's go tell her our news. She has been waiting to hear the outcome of our meeting." Mr. Wheatley held out his arm. Together he and Phillis walked up the stairs.

Mrs. Wheatley died shortly afterward, but Phillis remained with the family. War loomed closer and closer. On April 18, 1775, Paul Revere spread the word: "The British are coming!" The war had begun. Phillis continued writing poems; however, there was no longer a market for poetry in war-torn America. Her health grew steadily worse. In December of 1784, Phillis Wheatley died at the age of thirty-one. She is still remembered today for her poetry and for her remarkable love of learning.

Cast

Narrator

Billy Dawes

Caleb

Dr. Warren

Paul Revere

Robert Newman

Rachel

Joshua Bentley

Tom Richardson

Colonel Conant

British soldier

A Dark Night

Steffi Adams

illustrated by Del Thompson and Paula Cheadle

Act I

Narrator: The moon had not yet risen on the night of April 18, 1775. Billy Dawes and a friend hurried through Boston. A cold wind tore at their clothing and reddened their cheeks. At the corner of Hanover Street the men stopped. The faint clanking of British weapons mingled with the dull thud of boots.

Billy Dawes: *(talking quietly)* Mark my words, Caleb, those soldiers are up to no good. Why would they be gathering at North Square after dark?

Caleb: *(whispering)* Surely Dr. Warren knows. I wonder why he sent for us.

Narrator: The two patriots glanced up and down the street. Then, sneaking in and out of the shadows to avoid the British soldiers, they made their way to the doctor's house. A small flicker of light fell on the men's faces as Dr. Warren opened the door a crack. Then, unbolting it, he let the two men in.

Dr. Warren: Come in, come in!

Billy Dawes: Sir, North Square is filled with British troops!

Dr. Warren: Yes, yes, I know. We must act now! Can one of you ride across the Neck tonight?

Caleb: That narrow strip of land? That's been occupied by British soldiers for a long time.

Dr. Warren: Yes, but that's the only land route out of the city. The British are making plans to march on Concord to seize our weapons. They are also expecting to find Samuel Adams and John Hancock and arrest them. It's up to you to warn them!

Billy Dawes: I can get across the Neck, sir. I've done plenty of odd jobs for the soldiers camped there. To them I'm just a harmless farmer. They won't think twice about letting me through.

Dr. Warren: *(turning to Caleb)* Young man, do you know where Paul Revere lives?

Caleb: His house faces North Square, I believe, sir.

Dr. Warren: Yes. Tell him I need to see him immediately. Now be off, both of you.

Narrator: The two men disappeared into the night. Darting along dark alleys, Caleb made his way to the Revere house. He knocked quietly on the door. The door opened just wide enough for him to recognize Paul Revere.

Caleb: *(speaking quickly and quietly)* Dr. Warren wants to see you immediately, Mr. Revere. The soldiers that gathered in North Square have gone down to the river.

Narrator: Then, without even stopping to put on an overcoat, Paul Revere let himself out the back door. He followed a crooked course to the doctor's house. The silver moon made the direct route too dangerous. Around ten o'clock he knocked on the doctor's door.

Dr. Warren: Come in, Paul. We must hurry. The British troops are rowing across the Charles River. What plans were you able to make on Sunday with the people at Charlestown?

Paul Revere: They are to watch the belfry tower at North Church. Robert Newman will light one lantern if the British are coming by land, two if they come by sea.

Dr. Warren: Good, good. Get the signal out. Then take your boat across the river. The Charlestown patriots will have a horse waiting for you. You must ride like the wind, warning patriots in every house and village to hide their ammunition. Billy Dawes is already on his way to Lexington by way of the Neck to warn Hancock and Adams. We can't count on his getting through. You must also try to warn them.

Narrator: The two men shook hands. Both knew it would be a dangerous ride.

Act II

Narrator: Paul Revere paused outside the doctor's house. Should he go home to get an overcoat first? Or should he get the signal message to Robert Newman? The message was more important. Turning quickly on his heels, Paul Revere headed toward Sheafe and Salem Streets. At the corner, a shadowy figure stepped out of the darkness.

Paul Revere: *(in a subdued voice)* Robert, is that you?

Robert Newman: *(quietly)* I thought you might come tonight, so I waited outside. What is the message for our Charlestown friends?

Paul Revere: The British are going by boat. They expect to be in Lexington before dawn.

Robert Newman: Then we must hurry. You can depend on me. Two if by sea—right?

Paul Revere: Right! And God bless our land.

Narrator: The two men hurried off, Robert Newman to the North Church, and Paul Revere to his home. Pulling on his overcoat and riding boots, Paul Revere looked from one family member to another. It might be the last time he saw them.

Paul Revere: Son, take care of things. Rachel, my sweet wife, pray for me. This message must get through.

Rachel: Ride well, Paul. May America be blessed by your courage.

Narrator: Paul Revere slipped out into the night, his mind occupied by the task that lay before him. His pace quickened as he approached the hiding place of his small boat. Two men looked up as they heard his footsteps.

Joshua Bentley: Paul, I've wrapped your oars in old rags to muffle the sounds.

Tom Richardson: Don't know whether it will do much good. The British ship *Somerset* sits in the middle of the river. With this full moon, it will be a miracle if we are not spotted by her crew.

Paul Revere: We'll trust God to take care of us. Did you see the lantern signal?

Joshua Bentley: You mean the two lanterns from North Church?

Tom Richardson: We saw them shine briefly. I hope Charlestown was watching.

Paul Revere: We'll know once we reach the other side. Let's get going.

Narrator: Without a sound, the boat left the safety of the shadows with the three patriots. Out into the deep waters, out under the bright light of the moon the small boat glided. Slowly, painstakingly, silently the men rowed with muffled oars. At last the shadows of the Charlestown bank welcomed them.

Joshua Bentley: May God speed you this night, Paul Revere!

Paul Revere: Take care, men.

Narrator: Paul Revere leaped onto the bank and hurried to the house of Colonel Conant, where a group of men waited for him. He knocked at the door.

Colonel Conant: Paul! Come in, quickly. We saw the lights from the North Church tower. Our men say the roads to Cambridge and Concord are patrolled by British soldiers.

Paul Revere: Have you heard anything?

Colonel Conant: Some of the officers have been asking the villagers for the location of Clark's house.

Paul Revere: That's where Sam Adams and John Hancock are staying! Dr. Warren was right!

Colonel Conant: They intend to arrest the two men.

Paul Revere: I must get through whether the roads are guarded or not.

Colonel Conant: Come, we have a horse for you, the best horse in Charlestown.

Narrator: Paul Revere hurried outside. Two men led a light-footed horse out of the shadows. Revere quickly adjusted the stirrups and checked the girth. Then he swung into the saddle.

Colonel Conant: Be careful! Watch for the patrols!

Narrator: With a wave of his hand, Paul Revere galloped away down the moonlit road. He had not gone far before he saw the glint of moonlight on rifles. Two British soldiers blocked the road.

British soldier: Halt! Who goes there?

Narrator: Paul Revere didn't answer. He dug his
heels into his horse's sides and turned sharply into
the open fields. One of the soldiers spurred his
horse after him.

British soldier: Halt! Halt, I say, in the name of
the king!

Narrator: Closer and closer the soldier came. The
hard breathing of his horse made chills chase
along Paul Revere's spine. Then, ahead of him, he
saw a pond. Kicking his horse, he headed straight
for it. At the last moment he veered sharply to the
left. The British soldier galloped on, not able to
stop. Down the muddy bank slid horse and rider.
Paul Revere grinned to himself, rode his horse

around the pond, and headed toward Lexington. At every farmhouse and village along the way he shouted his message.

Paul Revere: The redcoats are coming! Awake! Awake!

Narrator: Windows flew open and nightcapped heads popped out. Men dressed quickly and grabbed their guns. Church bells pealed out the message. Meanwhile, Paul Revere rode hard for Lexington to warn Sam Adams and John Hancock so that the British would not find them.

As for the British, their surprise attack became a disaster. American minutemen, hiding in bushes by the side of the road, took easy aim at the soldiers marching in straight rows. The British army finally retreated and raced back for the safety of Boston. The War for Independence had begun.

Robert Hillyer

Lullaby

illustrated by Bob Reynolds

The long canoe
Toward the shadowy shore,
One . . . two . . .
Three . . . four . . .
The paddle dips,
Turns in the wake,
Pauses, then
Forward again,
Water drips
From the blade to the lake,
Nothing but that,
No sound of wings;
The owl and bat
Are velvet things.
No wind awakes,
No fishes leap,
No rabbits creep
Among the brakes.

The long canoe
At the shadowy shore,
One . . . two . . .
Three . . . four . . .
A murmur now
Under the prow
Where rushes bow
To let us through.
One . . . two . . .
Upon the shore,
Three . . . four . . .
Upon the lake,
No one's awake,
No one's awake,
One . . .
Two . . .
No one,
Not even
You.

Captured!

Steffi Adams

illustrated by Del Thompson

At Boonesborough in the summer of 1776, corn grew tall, apple and peach trees stood in neat rows, and chickens pecked busily at the ground around the log cabins. There had been no Indian attacks since December. Sunday afternoon was peaceful and hot. The water of the Kentucky River flowed past the settlement, cool and inviting.

"Indians!"

The canoe rocked gently as Jemima Boone dipped her sore foot into the cool water. "This feels good," she said with a sigh. "Let's paddle a little farther downstream."

"Should we?" asked sixteen-year-old Betsey Callaway. "Our daddies told us not to go too far downstream."

"Oh, I know why you are worried. You don't want to miss Samuel Henderson when he comes courting," Jemima said. She lifted her foot out of the water and inspected the jagged cut on the bottom. "I'll never walk barefoot in cane stubble again."

"Betsey wouldn't go barefoot. She wouldn't leave her good shoes at home," said Fanny Callaway, who was two years younger than her sister. "She wants to look like a city girl for her husband to be."

Betsey kept paddling. "Just wait until you meet someone you like," she told the two younger girls.

"Daddy says I'm too young to have a sweetheart," Jemima said.

"Your sister is my age," Betsey replied. "She's been married for more than a year. You'll change your mind soon enough."

"I don't want to think about that now," Jemima replied. "Let's sing."

At Jemima's suggestion the three girls began singing their favorite hymns. As they sang, Betsey's and Fanny's paddles kept time with the music. Slowly the canoe floated downstream.

The last hymn ended just as Fanny spotted colorful wildflowers on the bank. "Let's pick some flowers," she said.

Jemima looked at the thick cane on the river's edge. Dark, forested hills rose behind the cane. "Let's turn back," she said uneasily. "We've gone too far. Daddy will be angry with us for being so careless."

Betsey and Fanny turned the canoe upstream. They paddled with all their might, but the current carried the canoe toward the canebrake. Suddenly five Indians burst from their hiding place among the canes. One Indian waded into the water and grabbed the buffalo-hide rope at the front of the canoe.

"Let us be!" Jemima screamed. "Put down that rope!"

172

As the Indian pulled the canoe toward the shore, Fanny tried to beat him off with her paddle, but it broke. All three girls were screaming with fear.

The other Indians quickly ran into the waist-deep water, clapping rough hands over the girls' mouths. They dragged the kicking, struggling girls through the water and up the bank.

When they were safely hidden in the cane, the Indians raised their knives and tomahawks. One of the warriors grabbed Betsey's dark hair.

"Pretty squaw," said the Indian. "No scream."

Betsey's eyes opened wide and her mouth closed tightly. Jemima's and Fanny's mouths also snapped shut.

The Indians rushed the girls through the cane and into the forest. By the time they reached high ground, Jemima had calmed down and was thinking fast. At the top of a hill she dug her bare heels into the hard earth and said loudly, "I won't take one more step. You can kill me if you wish. Walking on this sore foot is worse than death."

"You think we no hear you?" the leader asked in his low voice. "You walk."

Jemima shook her head, crossed her arms, and sat down. "I'm not taking another step on this sore foot."

The Indian soldiers waved their tomahawks, but Jemima would not budge. Finally the leader made a sign. Two Indians handed their extra moccasins to Jemima and Fanny.

"Put on moccasins," said the Indian leader.

Jemima and Fanny quickly laced up their borrowed moccasins. As Jemima stood up, three warriors pulled out knives and stepped toward the girls.

"Squaws no run," they said as they cut off the girls' long skirts at their knees.

"Oh, no! This is my best dress," Betsey cried. "You've ruined it!"

"Long journey . . . we walk fast," the Indian said.

"Well, I won't run through the woods and canebrakes like this," Jemima said, looking at her bare legs. "The underbrush and briars will tear up my legs."

The leader made a sign to the warrior who had picked up the torn pieces of the girls' skirts.

"Wrap legs," he said.

As she wrapped the cloth around her legs to protect them, Jemima wondered about the leader. "The other Indians are Shawnees, but he is a Cherokee," she thought. "He speaks much better English than the others. Who is he? Where have I seen him before?"

Suddenly Jemima remembered the Cherokee chief, Hanging Maw, who had often visited the Boone cabin in North Carolina. This chief had brought her pretty shells and feathers. He had eaten bread and stew with her family.

"Do you remember me, Hanging Maw?" Jemima asked the chief. "When I was a little girl, you brought me gifts. I'm Jemima Boone, Daniel Boone's daughter."

"You Boone's girl?" asked Hanging Maw.

"Yes," Jemima replied.

Hanging Maw pointed to Betsey and Fanny. "And they too?"

"Yes," Jemima lied. She hoped that Hanging Maw would treat the Callaway girls better if he thought they were Boones.

Hanging Maw laughed. "How de do!" he said, as he shook each girl's hand. "Well, we do pretty good for this time."

The Shawnees also shook hands with the girls. "How de do! How de do!"

"Come now," said Hanging Maw. "We go."

Traveling North

Any hope of being released disappeared as Hanging Maw took Jemima's arm. Two of the Shawnees grabbed Betsey and Fanny. Those Indians and two others entered the nearby canebrake from different spots. Jemima knew that meant the Indians were leaving five trails through the canebrake to confuse her father. "Will I see him again?" she wondered. "Will I see any of my family again?"

Jemima gasped for breath as Hanging Maw pulled her along faster. The tall, thick canes shut out most of the light and air. Snakes sometimes crawled near her feet, and mosquitoes buzzed around her hot face all the time.

At last Hanging Maw pulled Jemima from the dry canebrake. Just ahead, the other Indians were waiting with Betsey and Fanny.

The Indians did not stop to rest. One warrior walked behind to guard the rear. The other four Indians led their captives down the middle of cool streams and across the dark hills.

Jemima remembered the things that her father had taught her. She noticed that the afternoon sun was in the west. She also studied the moss and vines that grew on the trees.

"Let's see," Jemima thought. "Moss grows on the dark north side of a tree, while thicker vines grow on the sunny south side."

When she knew the direction they were walking, Jemima asked, "May we have something to eat?"

Hanging Maw stopped and gave the girls some of the dried meat from his pouch. "Eat," he said.

"We have been walking north all afternoon. Where are you taking us?" Jemima asked as she bit down on the chewy meat.

"Shawnee towns . . . north," Hanging Maw replied. "Pretty squaws of Wide Mouth Boone will make good wives for Shawnee warriors."

With these words, Hanging Maw returned to the front of the column. He led his small group through more canebrakes, always making more than one trail.

When they were back under the trees, Betsey and Fanny walked beside Jemima. They held her up when she stumbled. Once Betsey whispered in despair, "How will our daddies find us?"

"Daddy is the best tracker in Kentucky," Jemima whispered back. "I am sure that he is trailing us. He knows that the Indians would kill us before they'd let white men take us. He will rescue us when it is safe."

The sun was beginning to go down when Hanging Maw stopped for the night near a gurgling mountain stream. Before the chief lay down, he tied the girls' arms together behind their backs and set each of them against a different tree.

"One end of thong tied to tree. We hold other end," said Hanging Maw. "Squaws no run."

"My foot hurts dreadfully, and you have bound my arms too tightly," Jemima said, almost in tears.

Hanging Maw pulled off Jemima's moccasin. The chief unwrapped his headband, rinsed it in the cool water, and washed Jemima's foot. Then he reached into his pouch.

"Good medicine," he said as he rubbed a mixture on Jemima's wound.

When he had spread the mixture evenly, Hanging Maw collected moss and bark from a nearby log. Carefully, he placed the cool moss over the wound. Then he wrapped the elm bark and his wet headband around Jemima's foot.

"Now sleep," said Hanging Maw.

"But what about this rope?" Jemima asked. "Won't you loosen it?"

"No," said Hanging Maw with a grunt. He picked up one end of the rope and lay down. The sky was dark now. Jemima couldn't see the other two girls, but she could hear a sob now and then that could not be muffled. Soon she heard Hanging Maw's heavy breathing. Jemima thought of her oldest brother, James, who had been killed by Indians three years before. One of the Indians who had killed James had even been a friend of the Boones, like Hanging Maw. The tears that Jemima had held back all day began to fall.

"Tears won't save us," she thought, blinking her eyes. Softly she began to hum "At Home with God Anywhere." "What will morning bring?" she wondered as owls hooted and wolves howled. "Will it bring Daddy or death?"

Leaving a Trail

When the first rays of the sun appeared over the mountain, the Indians untied the sleepy girls.

"May we wash?" Jemima asked.

Hanging Maw nodded. "Squaws no run," he warned, patting his rifle.

The three girls walked the short distance to the stream. They cupped their hands and lifted the refreshing water to their lips. When they had finished drinking, they splashed themselves with the cool water.

Suddenly Jemima plopped down on the bank. "Help me wash my foot," she said in a loud voice.

The girls carefully unwrapped Hanging Maw's bandage. Then Betsey dipped her handkerchief into the water and began washing the wound. "It looks much better this morning," she said.

"It feels much better," Jemima said softly. "Keep washing my foot and listen closely. I have a plan."

"What is it?" asked Betsey.

"I'm sure that the men are close behind us," Jemima replied. "We must leave signs for them to follow."

"How?" asked Fanny.

"Fanny, you break twigs," said Jemima. "Betsey, dig your heels into the mud and drop pieces of your handkerchief."

"But what if the Indians see us?" Betsey asked as she finished washing Jemima's foot.

Before Jemima could answer, Hanging Maw said, "Pretty squaws. Come."

Jemima wrapped the headband around her foot, put on her moccasin, and stood up. "Watch yourselves," she whispered.

Once again, the Indians made five trails. But on this morning the girls smiled to themselves. They had a plan!

As they walked along the trail, the girls left signs. Betsey dug her heels into the damp earth. Fanny lagged behind and broke twigs. Jemima fell into thorn bushes, letting sharp thorns snag pieces of her dress.

Suddenly the Indian at the rear pushed past the girls. He carried small pieces of cloth.

Hanging Maw stared at the torn spots in Jemima's dress. "What's this?" he asked.

"My foot hurts," Jemima replied. "Sometimes when I hold on to a bush, a thorn snags my dress."

Hanging Maw said nothing, but he and the other Indians began watching the girls more carefully. When Betsey again stepped in mud, they wiped away her heelprints and broke off her wooden heels. When Fanny broke twigs, they bent the twigs in the opposite direction. When Jemima snagged her dress, they picked the cloth off the thorns.

All morning the girls tried to leave signs. Sometimes, when they were very clever, they left signs that the Indians' sharp eyes missed.

Once Hanging Maw saw Betsey press the sole of her shoe into the damp earth. As he bent over to wipe away the print, she tossed a piece of her tattered skirt under a bush.

Jemima also left many signs. During the morning she often screamed loudly and fell into the bushes, breaking hundreds of twigs. "Oh! My poor foot!" she would say when the Indians waved their tomahawks.

Clumsy Riders

At noon the Indians found a stray pony in the woods. Hanging Maw slipped a rope over the pony's head and then lifted Jemima onto the pony's back.

"Pretty squaw ride," he said, as he led the pony over the narrow trail.

Jemima grabbed the pony's thick mane. She wobbled from side to side as the pony trotted behind Hanging Maw. When the Indians were not watching, she pinched the pony.

"Help! I'm falling!" Jemima shouted as the pony stood up on its hind legs. A second later she slid to the ground.

The Indians laughed heartily at such a "clumsy" girl. They picked her up, brushed her off, and set her back on the pony.

At the next hill Jemima slid off again. This time the Indians smiled weakly. Hanging Maw picked up Jemima and set her on the pony. At his signal, one of the warriors set Fanny in front of her. Another warrior set Betsey behind her.

"Pretty squaws sit on pony," Hanging Maw said.

Jemima smiled. A short time later all three girls screamed and tumbled to the ground.

The Indians frowned and grumbled among themselves. At last one warrior sat on the pony. He grabbed the pony's mane and pressed his knees tightly against the animal's sides.

"Watch," said Hanging Maw to the girls.

Jemima laughed as the warrior rode around and around with his toes almost touching the ground.

"I can do that," she said.

Jemima grabbed the pony's mane. She pressed her knees against the pony's sides.

"Good," said Hanging Maw.

Jemima bit her lip as the pony trotted. For ten minutes she wobbled from side to side. Then she pinched the pony again. Jemima flew backwards through the air and landed on an Indian.

The pony finally grew impatient with the strange people around him. The next time Jemima pinched him and slid down his back, he snorted and bit Hanging Maw.

"Go," said Hanging Maw. He slapped the angry pony and sent it galloping through the woods.

Jemima carefully picked herself up from the bush where she had fallen. "Surely Daddy will find us now," she thought as she rubbed the bruises that covered her body.

Early Tuesday morning the Indians and their captives crossed a small stream. An hour later one of the Indians shot a buffalo and cut out the hump.

"We cook at next water," said Hanging Maw.

"That means they'll make a fire," Jemima thought. Her heart sank. "Why are the Indians so careless today?"

"Have you heard the Indians talking about Boonesborough?" Fanny whispered. "They are saying that many Indians are supposed to have attacked the fort."

"Something must have happened," Jemima replied. "Daddy should have rescued us by now."

The girls walked the next few miles in silence. As the sun rose higher and higher in the sky, their spirits sank lower and lower. "The men are not coming for us," they thought.

At noon the girls and the hungry Indians waded down a mountain stream until they came to a small creek. "Sit," said Hanging Maw to the girls.

Betsey leaned against a giant oak tree. She sighed and slowly lowered herself to the hard earth.

Fanny and Jemima crumpled to the ground. They laid their heads in Betsey's lap. Tears trickled down their dirty cheeks onto the torn folds of Betsey's best dress.

Rescue

When the girls were settled, the Indians began fixing their noon meal. Hanging Maw walked to the stream to fill a kettle with water. One Indian stood guard on a small mound in the rear. The other Indians gathered wood, kindled a fire, and put a stick through the buffalo hump.

At first the guard stood on his mound and searched the bushes for enemies. Then, when the meat began sizzling, he put down his rifle and strolled toward the fire.

Jemima watched the guard squat down beside the fire and begin sewing the rips in his moccasins. "I wish that I had obeyed Daddy," she said to the other girls. "I'm sorry we ever paddled down that river. I don't want to live like an Indian for the rest of my life."

Suddenly a shot rang out. Jemima sat up just as the guard dropped his moccasins and tumbled to the ground.

More shots whistled through the camp. The wounded guard crawled into a nearby canebrake.

"That's Daddy!" cried Jemima as the rifles cracked.

The Indians around the fire dashed for the canebrake. The men in the bushes yelled, "Run, gals, run!"

Jemima jumped up, screaming with joy. She ran toward the men in the bushes. Betsey and Fanny followed at her heels.

The girls had run only a few feet when Daniel Boone shouted, "Fall down!"

Instantly, the three girls fell flat on their stomachs. Just as they hit the ground, a tomahawk sailed over Betsey's head. Knives fell on all sides.

When the Indians retreated, the men rushed into the camp, and Jemima ran into her father's arms.

Samuel Henderson scooped Betsey up into a hug.

While the men made sure that the girls had not been harmed, the crashing and rustling in the canebrake stopped.

"The Indians are escaping," some men said. "It shouldn't be hard to capture them. At least two Indians were wounded."

"They have left behind everything except one rifle," said Daniel Boone as he hugged Jemima. "Let them go. We've got our girls back."

Fanny asked, "Where's Daddy?"

"We knew the Indians would take you north," Daniel explained. "He and some horsemen rode straight to the Licking River. They are waiting to ambush the Indians. When they see that we have rescued you, they will join us."

While Daniel Boone talked, Betsey stared at Samuel. Finally she asked, "What's wrong with your beard, Samuel?"

"I had shaved only half of my beard when I heard your screams on Sunday," Samuel said with a laugh. "I haven't shaved since then."

"I was asleep when you girls screamed," Daniel Boone added. "I followed you in my bare feet and Sunday clothes. I didn't have my moccasins until the women sent our hunting clothes."

"Is Mama safe?" Jemima asked. "We thought the Indians had attacked Boonesborough. Hanging Maw boasted that many Indians were on their way to the fort."

"Everyone was safe when we left," said her father. "I hope the Indians have not attacked since then."

"What took you so long?" Fanny asked.

Daniel pushed his felt hat to the back of his head. "We have had a hard time tracking you," he explained.

"The Indians left behind many trails and false signs. We finally decided to head straight north."

"Did you see our signs?" asked Jemima.

"Yes, we often came upon a broken twig, a scrap of cloth, or a heelprint. When we saw your signs we knew that we were on the right trail," Daniel said. "I was sure that my Mima knew how to mark a trail."

Jemima smiled at her father's praise.

Now that the girls were safe, many of the men wanted to hurry back to Boonesborough to make sure that their families had not been attacked.

"We must finish building the fort," they said.

Daniel looked at the tired girls and rubbed his chin. "The girls have not slept much in two nights," he said. "We will walk a short distance and then make camp. The men we left behind should be able to hold the fort until we return."

"Thank you, Daddy," Jemima said. "I'm sorry that I disobeyed you. You told me not to go far downstream."

"I'm so glad that you're safe. I forgive you," said Daniel.

"I will never forget these last three days," Jemima replied. "They will always remind me to obey."

Sooner or Later

Becky Davis

illustrated by
Del Thompson
and Mary Ann Lumm

Wanting to Go

A gust of cold wind whipped the edge of the tablecloth and swept flames up the stone chimney.

"Close the door quickly, Matthew!" Ma snatched a pot from the flames.

Matthew kicked the door closed behind him and clumped to the wood box. He dropped the firewood into the box and hung his coat and hat on the peg by the door. A low whine and scratching on the door made him stop and look at his father.

"Let them in, Matthew," said Pa.

When Matthew opened the door, two coonhounds charged into the room. The older dog trotted over to Pa and sat down. The younger dog dashed to the fireplace where Samantha sat on the floor. She hugged him around his neck and climbed up on his back.

She pulled on his long, floppy ears. "Giddap, Sooner!" The young coonhound wiggled and turned to lick her face.

Matthew looked at the older coonhound at his father's knee. "Old Blue's been acting funny all day, Pa. Kinda restless. Maybe he smells Indians."

"Indians!" Rebecca dropped her knitting.

"Injins!" Samantha slid off Sooner's back.

"Matthew, don't scare your sisters like that," said Ma.

"He may be right, Ma." Pa rubbed Old Blue's head. "Blue has a way of knowing when danger is about. There was an Indian uprising down the river just a couple of weeks ago."

"The winter makes life hard for the Indians." Ma stirred the fire.

"It has been a hard winter." Pa laid his hand on Old Blue's head. "Even the animals can't find enough to eat."

195

Old Blue got up and padded quietly to the window, whimpering. Pa followed him, opened the wooden shutter, and peered out into the twilight.

"Don't see a thing," he said. "But Matthew, we'd better take Blue and have a look around."

"May we take Sooner, too?" Matthew did not look up. "After all, he's younger than Old Blue and—"

"Younger!" Pa looked at Sooner. "He's younger than Blue all right! But he's almost two years old, and he's still nothing but an overgrown puppy. He's afraid of his own shadow and too busy playing to learn anything. You'd never know he's Blue's son. I might as well just get rid of him."

"Oh, no, Pa!" Samantha threw her arms around Sooner's neck. "Please let us keep Sooner! Please!" Two heads turned toward Pa, and two pairs of brown eyes looked at him.

Pa did not smile. "We'll have to wait and see. But while Blue is warning us of danger, Sooner sits by the fireplace with a foolish grin on his face. Sooner or later that dog will have to grow up!"

Matthew remembered how Sooner had gotten his name. Pa had picked him from a litter of pups and said, "Sooner or later, we'll have another Blue."

Samantha, only three at the time, had touched the little puppy and said, "Sooner." Pa had laughed, and "Sooner" became the puppy's name. Now Sooner was no longer a puppy, but he still hadn't lived up to his name.

Matthew looked at Sooner and sighed. "If we count on you to be another Blue," he thought, "looks like it will be later, not sooner."

Pa took his gun from the shelf. Matthew pulled on his coat and whistled. Both dogs came.

"No, Sooner." Samantha pulled at Sooner's tail. "Stay here with me!" He turned, and she hugged him around the neck again.

"Ma, don't you worry; the Lord will protect us."
Pa put his arm around her. "Just pray for us while we
are gone."

"We will." Ma leaned her head against his shoulder.

Pa kissed her gently on the cheek. Then with Old
Blue pulling hard on the leash, he followed him out
the door. Matthew closed the door behind them.

Rebecca turned to Ma. "Do you think it really is
Indians, Ma?"

"Only the Lord knows, dear," Ma replied. "But we
don't need to be afraid. God will protect us." Ma sat
down in the rocking chair. She pulled Samantha into
her lap and put her arm around Rebecca. "Let's ask
God to take care of us."

When they were finished praying, Ma kissed
Samantha and put her down. "Now let's get to work,"
she said. "While we're working, we'll quote some
promises from the Bible."

As they worked quietly, they took turns quoting
verses. From time to time the girls looked toward the
door. It seemed as if Pa and Matthew had been gone
a long time.

Needed to Stay

Finally Ma opened the wooden shutter a crack. The girls crowded behind her. Outside all was dark and quiet except for the gusts of wind that swept snowflakes past the window.

"It's snowing," Ma said. "Since there'll be no tracks to follow, Pa and Matthew should be back soon."

As Ma closed the shutter, they heard a horrible howl from the woods.

"Indians!" Rebecca threw herself into Ma's arms. Samantha began to cry. Sooner slunk back against the hearth and whimpered.

"The Lord will protect us, children," said Ma, but her voice trembled. "Rebecca, say another verse."

Rebecca lifted her face from Ma's shoulder. "What about Psalm 46:1? 'God is our refuge and strength, a very present help in trouble.' "

"That's a good one." Ma smoothed Rebecca's hair with her hand. "How about Psalm 91:11: 'He shall give his angels charge over thee, to keep thee in all thy ways.' "

The same howl—half shriek, half roar—came again from outside.

"It's closer this time!" Rebecca hugged Ma tighter.

"We must trust the Lord, girls." Ma gave Rebecca a quick hug and let go. "Now, Rebecca, help me stir the stew. And, Samantha, you set the table. We'll have something hot to eat as soon as the men get home."

Rebecca began to stir the stew. Sooner trotted over to the table and lay on the floor close to Samantha as she set the table. He lay still, panting, watching the door. A low growl came from his throat. "What is it, Sooner?" Samantha knelt down beside him. "Is it Injins?"

"Maybe he hears Pa and Matthew coming home." Rebecca stopped stirring.

"We'll know soon enough." Mother took the spoon from Rebecca's hand. "You go help Samantha finish—"

Just then Sooner leaped toward the door, barking furiously. Standing on his hind legs, he pawed at the door.

"Rebecca, quick, bring me the gun." Ma tried to pull Sooner away from the door. "Down, Sooner, down."

Sooner pulled harder toward the door, barking and growling.

Ma finally pushed him back, lifted the bar, and opened the door. Sooner leaped out the doorway in a blur.

Rebecca and Samantha crowded into the doorway behind their mother. "What is it, Ma?"

In the clearing just below the house stood the dark figure of a large cat, poised to spring. In a moment Sooner threw himself on the mountain lion. Over and over they rolled. The beast tore at Sooner with his claws. Sooner grabbed the cat by its neck.

"Don't shoot Sooner, Ma. Please, don't shoot Sooner." Rebecca pressed up behind Ma.

"Get back inside the house." Ma stepped to the edge of the porch. She peered down the barrel of the gun trying to get the mountain lion in her sights. The animals twisted and turned. She could not be sure which one she would hit. She fired. Both animals fell.

Samantha grabbed her mother's skirts. "Did you kill Sooner, Ma?"

"I hope not, Samantha." Ma strained to see. "But I guess we'd better go find out."

Ma cradled the gun in the crook of her arm and took Samantha's hand. Rebecca followed behind.

Just before they reached the clearing, they heard voices and Old Blue's bark.

"Pa and Matthew!" Samantha tugged at her mother's hand. Old Blue bounded past them.

Matthew was not far behind. "We heard a shot. What happened?"

Ma could only point at the fallen animals. Matthew ran down to where Sooner lay. Samantha followed him.

Rebecca grabbed her father's hand. "It's a mountain lion, Pa. Sooner knocked him down, and then Ma shot him."

"I'm afraid I hit Sooner too." Ma walked toward the fallen dog. Just as she reached him, he rolled over and struggled to his feet.

"He's all right, Ma, look." Samantha tried to hug Sooner. He fell at her feet.

"He's hurt bad, Samantha." Matthew put his hand on his little sister's shoulder. "We'll have to be careful."

Pa knelt beside the wounded dog and ran his hands over his body. Old Blue stood growling over the dead mountain lion.

"Looks like you hit the right one, Ma." Pa smiled. "But it looks like Old Blue wants to take all the credit." Pa stood up. "Matthew, get an old blanket from the barn, and we'll carry Sooner up to the house. Ma and the girls can bandage his wounds while we skin this old cat."

When the family finally sat down to eat the stew, Ma explained what had happened. Pa let out a low whistle. "So that's what was bothering Old Blue. The Lord kept Sooner here to protect you. I guess he's a better dog than I thought."

"Sooner's going to be all right, isn't he, Pa?" asked Samantha.

Pa looked at the young coonhound's bandages. He shook his head. "I just don't know, Samantha, I just don't know."

At that moment Sooner lifted his head and thumped his tail against the floor. Pa knelt beside him and gently rubbed his head. "Now that's a good sign." Sooner nuzzled his hand. Pa stroked Sooner's ears. "Guess you fooled me, didn't you, boy? Looks like you did grow up sooner than I expected."

Creatures
Great and
Small

from MICE

of the

WESTING WIND

BOOK TWO

Tim Davis / illustrated by Tim Davis

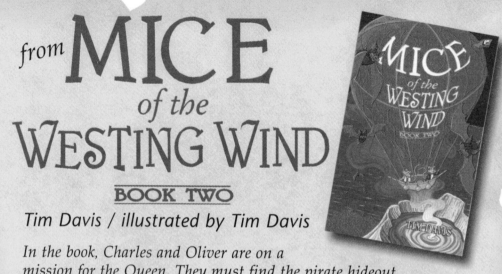

In the book, Charles and Oliver are on a mission for the Queen. They must find the pirate hideout in the Cattibean Sea. In Chapter One, they were stranded on an island after being discovered on the pirate ship, the Westing Wind. *They had escaped by jumping overboard. Now they must find a way off the island so they can finish their mission.*

fo

"What might work?" asked Oliver.

A Westing Wind blows toward the West.

Boofo

"What might work?" asked Oliver.

"A balloon, of course," said Charles. "With a boat hanging from it!"

Oliver twisted his head. "It looks like a flowerpot to me."

"You're looking at it upside down," said Charles. "Come over here!"

Oliver stepped around the drawing to the other side. "It looks wonderful, Charles, but where are we going to find a balloon?"

"We'll build it!" exclaimed Charles. "I've been looking at the trees and vines in the forest, and I've seen some really big leaves. We could sew them together. In fact, I think we can find everything we need, right here!"

"That's nice," Oliver said slowly. "But this looks like something that could take *weeks* to build. And we've already lost a day. If we don't start after the *Westing Wind* soon, we'll be hopelessly behind them."

208

Charles didn't say anything for a minute. Then he sat down on the sand and put his head in his paws. "I guess you're right."

Oliver put an arm around his friend and patted his back. "Sorry to burst your balloon, Charles," he said. "Why don't you come over and get something to eat? Maybe it will help you feel better."

"Thanks, old chap. I guess I might as well."

Charles stood up and tossed his scribbling stick toward a clump of tall grass.

Thwap. A familiar-looking tongue snapped the stick out of midair.

Oliver grinned. "I think he deserves to eat something better than that," he whispered. He picked up a red berry and threw it in the same direction.

Thwap—came the tongue again.

Then Charles joined in the fun.

Thwap. Thwap. Thwap!

Soon they had thrown half their breakfast into the tall grass, laughing all the while. When the berries stopped flying, an orange-and-black tree frog hopped into the clearing. He had berry juice all over his face. "Juicy flies," croaked the frog. "Thanks!" His long tongue licked his face clean.

Oliver giggled. "Glad you liked them."

"Like the hole?" asked the frog.

Charles paused. "Oh, yes—the hole—the cave. Thank you for telling us about it."

"Good hole," croaked the frog. "But not for me. No bugs."

"That's fine with us," Oliver said. He scratched at a mosquito bite.

Charles sat down on a rock. "Do you know Emilio?" he asked.

"Uh-huh. Good friends." The frog smiled and hopped closer.

"All good bats . . . they eat 'em high . . . we eat 'em low."

"Uh . . ." Oliver looked puzzled.

"The mosquitoes," said Charles.

"Yes, of course," said Oliver.

"Everybody," said the frog, "works together. Everybody . . . knows his place—Island rule."

"Indeed?" said Charles politely. "By the way, I'm Charles, and this is Oliver."

"Boofo," announced the frog.

Charles and Oliver looked at each other and then at the frog.

"Pardon me?" Charles asked.

"Boofo," the frog said again. He pointed to himself.

Charles and Oliver looked at the frog and then at each other. "Oh!" they said together.

"Boofo," said Oliver, "do you remember the sea dogs?"

At the mention of sea dogs, Boofo began to frown. "Don't like 'em," he croaked. "Too big mouths . . . too big feet . . . too much smoke."

Oliver scratched his head.

"Oh," Charles looked at Oliver. "You mean they made a lot of noise, trampled down the forest, and built big fires on the beach . . ."

"Uh-huh," croaked Boofo. "No give . . . all take . . . whole Island glad . . . to see 'em go . . . would've helped 'em . . . go sooner!"

Oliver sat up straight, and his whiskers twitched with excitement. He smiled at Charles. Then he turned to the tree frog again. "Did you mean the *whole Island* would have helped them go?"

"Uh-huh," croaked the frog. "Everybody . . . work together . . ."

"And would you work together," interrupted Oliver, "to make sure those sea dogs *never* come back here again?"

"Uh-huh," Boofo croaked eagerly.

"Yippee!" shouted Oliver.

Charles grinned, but Boofo looked puzzled.

"Listen, Boofo," said Charles. "If you and the rest of the Island creatures help us build a balloon, we'll do our best to keep those sea dogs far, far away from here!"

"If you build it . . . they will not come?"

"Right, Boofo!" said Oliver. "Will you help us?"

"We will build it," croaked the frog. "I tell others!"

"Yippee!"

"C'mon," said Charles. "Let's get things ready for our crew of helpers!"

All Together

"The biggest palm leaves you can find," said Oliver to several crabs. "And thank you for coming to help!"

"Give and take—it's the Island rule," replied one crab.

Volunteers came to Charles and Oliver by the dozens. The mice assigned them each a particular job to do.

Crabs would trim large leaves to size. Needle-nosed hummingbirds would sew the leaves together. Tree frogs would gather bark and vines.

Then they would begin building a gondola that would hang underneath the balloon. Everyone worked together, just as Boofo had said they would.

But the bats rested. Charles had a special job for them that night.

"Excellent, Boofo," said Charles. "That bark will do just fine!"

Soon a hopping line of bark-laden tree frogs returned from the forest. "Everybody . . . work together," they croaked in chorus. "Everybody . . . do his part!"

Meanwhile, other Island creatures prepared food for a great feast. Oliver smelled things cooking that he'd never smelled before or even dreamed about.

"As they say—" chuckled a jolly gecko, "—you are welcome to come, but forbidden to go—at least not without *eating* first!"

By midafternoon, the balloon had started to take shape. Charles had laid it out on a shady part of the beach. Crabs brought fresh supplies of cut leaves, and hummingbird seamstresses flitted back and forth.

Oliver brought more threadlike vines for the sewing, and then he inspected the stitching they had done.

"Marvelous work!" he exclaimed. "This embroidery is as fine as you would see on the Queen's own robes!" He carried some nectar to the thirsty hummingbirds.

Charles watched over the construction of the gondola. Boofo and his crew of tree frogs followed the mouse's design with great care. They even contributed some slime to make it watertight.

"Excellent work!" exclaimed Charles. "I believe we'll finish by sunset!"

"Uh-huh," said Boofo.

Hours later, as the sun sank into the sea, they finished the marvelous balloon. The big, leafy-green bag lay neatly on the sand. Vines connected it to the bark-and-slime gondola, which was rimmed with little green sandbags. The gondola was packed with all manner of supplies: nuts, water, and even a pair of soft, grass-filled leafy pillows.

"Thank you," said Charles.

"Thank you *very* much," said Oliver.

"Give first," croaked Boofo. "Island rule."

"We do thank you *all*," said Oliver, looking at the Island creatures gathered round.

"Leaving soon?" asked Boofo sadly.

"When the bats come out," replied Charles. He patted the tree frog's back.

"Can't leave yet," shouted the jolly gecko. "It's time to feast!"

Dozens of bowls had been set in line on the beach, and they contained foods of every imaginable color and texture. The delicious smells made Oliver's nose twitch with anticipation.

"We shall begin!" said Boofo.

Oliver began. At times he wasn't sure *what* he was eating, but he took a taste from each bowl. Everything was an Island delicacy! How could he refuse even *one* bite?

"I wonder if there are any *mosquitoes* in this food?" he asked Charles quietly.

"Keep an eye on what the frogs eat."

The flavor of the food was made even better by the flavor of Island music.

Tree frogs chanted a chorus, and the hummingbirds blended in. The crabs snapped their pincers in time. The gecko sang and patted out a rhythm on his collection of shell drums.

"Are you sure we should leave?" Oliver whispered to Charles.

Charles nodded. "I know it's tempting to stay, but . . ."

Oliver smiled and said, "I know! We must do our *duty!*"

"For Her Majesty . . ." started Charles.

"And for England!" finished Oliver.

Charles winked at Oliver. "Sort of like the Island rule, eh?"

They listened to the music until it was interrupted by the sounds of flapping wings and high-pitched squeaks. The bats had come to do their part. It was time to go.

Whoosh!

The cloud of approaching bats darkened the moonlight as they flapped their way down to the beach.

"Emilio must have brought every bat on the Island!" said Oliver.

"We may need them all," said Charles.

The bats squeaked greetings to their friends and sampled leftovers from the feast. Then they inspected the balloon.

"Great mosqueeeto-mush," said Emilio, still smacking his lips. "Eees that your wife's recipeeee, Boofo?"

The tree frog smiled and grunted, "Uh-huh."

Oliver gulped.

"Gather 'round," called Emilio. "Get een your places, all bats!"

The bats surrounded the balloon, finding their proper toeholds. Charles and Oliver said their last farewells to the other Island creatures. Then the two mice climbed into their gondola and waved once more.

218

Emilio counted. "One, two, threeeeee!"

All the bats flapped together—and they lifted the green balloon up from the beach, carrying it up into the air. The gondola jerked up after them. Oliver tightened his grip on the side, and kept waving to their friends.

"Good-bye, everyone! Good-bye!"

As they crossed over the forest, Oliver lost sight of the creatures on the beach. Now they were headed toward the great mountain and its hot, bubbling water. There the bats would start them on their way.

The force of the bats' flapping wings soon sent currents of warm, moist air back into the mice's faces. Droplets formed on their whiskers again, just as they had when Emilio flew them over the mountain. Although the balloon was still folded, it soon began to ripple in the air currents.

"Isn't it about time to open it up?" asked Oliver.

"Not yet," answered Charles. "We want to get the hottest air in it that we can—before the bats let us go. So we're going right over the top of the mountain."

"Dear me," said Oliver. "I hope they can control it in that blast."

"Better get a good grip, Oliver. We could be in for a rough ride!"

"*Now* you tell me," said Oliver.

They drew closer and closer to the upper edge of the mountain. The bats put their heads down, flying hard against the updraft.

"Open thee balloon!" called Emilio. "Now!"

Several bats quickly changed their position.

Whooosh, whoosh.

Two bats lost their grip and were lifted high into the sky above.

"Carefulleeee, carefulleeee," cried Emilio. "Don't let go teel the balloon eez full!"

"Hope they can keep it down long enough," said Charles.

Oliver clung to the side of the gondola with all his might. It bounced in the swirling air. He didn't dare to look up . . . or down.

"Looks full from here!" called Charles.

"On thee count of threee, reeleeease thee balloon," called Emilio. "One—two—threeeee!"

All at once, the bats let go. The balloon lurched upward as the bats scattered in every direction.

"Good-byeeeeeeee!" Emilio's fading farewell came on the warm breeze.

Soon Oliver's heart stopped its heavy thumping, and he could look around.

A gentle wind had caught the balloon and was sending it out over the dark blue sea.

"Welcome to come, but forbidden to go, " Charles said softly. He watched the Island shrink into the distance.

The gondola rocked gently. Oliver peeked cautiously over the side. "This would be rather nice," he said, "*if* we didn't have sea dogs to capture."

Charles nodded. "And perhaps Captain Tabby to rescue."

Oliver sighed. "I think I'll take a nap while it's still quiet." He settled down on his pillow and watched the stars go by until everything faded into darkness.

Chickadee Winter

Dawn L. Watkins
illustrated by Gabriela Dellosso

Chickadee Winter
Dawn L. Watkins
illustrated by
Gabriela Dellosso

Not Like Home

We got there just after the snow.

It was not like home at all.
It was too cold. Too quiet.
And I missed my friends.

New Mexico had been all the colors of warm:
Red, orange, yellow, gold-brown, cinnamon.
When the sun went down,
the whole world was bronze.

Nora, my sister, said, "Look! clouds!"
And blew into the air—
air so cold it made my teeth ache.
Little cumulus clouds floated a moment,
then vanished.

And "Look! Feathers!" She pointed out
white, angled frost on windows.
I never knew that cold could paint on glass.
And I did not know of any bird
with such sharp white feathers.
Roadrunners have grey-brown tails
with only a few flecks of white.

But I saw here only
whiteness stretching out forever,
and at night I felt only keen-eyed stars
watching down and down.

"Listen!" Nora said, at the *scrunch-grunch*
scrunch-grunch, scrunch-grunch of our boots.
"And listen," she said,
at the beady repeats of the chickadee.
    Chick-a-dee-dee-dee.
    Chick-a-dee-dee-dee.

I heard only the tall silence of the pines.

Nora ran to the feeder
to make the chickadees fly.
And up they flew in a thrum of wings
to the safety of the hemlocks.
"Chick-a-dee-dee-dee,"
they said down to us.

When Grandfather came out of the house,
the birds swirled toward him like a dust storm.
And it made him smile.

Somehow I understood why they did that.

A Winter Man

We ate our suppers
with Grandfather and Grandmother.
There were never tacos or pizza.
We had beef stew and chicken and dumplings—
mounds of something like bread,
gooey on the outside
and dry as the desert inside.
I could only hope that the kitchen
in the farmhouse we bought
would get remodeled soon.

My mother said, "I grew up here."
My father said, "Come spring,
we'll plant a garden."
My sister said, "How high will the snow get?"
I said nothing.
If you don't have anything good to say,
Don't say anything at all—that's the rule.

The only good thing was Grandfather.
He was a winter man.
His hair was white and smooth like a drift;
his eyes were ice blue like a Christmas sky.

He was always quiet, like the pines in the snow.

I crunched behind him to the barn.
Scruncha-grunch. Scruncha-grunch.
I shadowed him when he milked the cows,
in the stillness of the barn,
and the cows snuffling
through their hay-dinners.

I helped him carry wood
and build fires in the fireplace.
I supposed that I would need to know
how to build a fire,
because evenings can get chilly in the West.

I stomped in his prints to the tops of hills.
I stood beside him when he looked
at next summer's trees.
He never asked me any questions.
He never told me how much better
this was than New Mexico.

Every morning and night
he fed the chickadees.
They flicked around him.

    Chick-a-dee-dee-dee.
    Chick-a-dee-dee-dee.

They darted at his cap
and the scoop he carried.

They sat on his hat.
They hung under the bill
and looked him in the eye.
They rode on the button.
They flew behind him
to the feeder.

Sometimes they came to the window
to look for him.
They flicked by, clamoring for attention.
Sometimes they even clicked the panes
with their beaks.
"Better go see what they want," he would say.

Nora asked him, "Why do they let you
come up to them,
but they fly away from me?"
He finished filling the feeders
and put the scoop away before he answered.

"They are used to me," he said.
"They just need a little more time;
they'll get used to you.
Things take some getting used to."

Then he looked at me.
I couldn't tell whether he wanted to see
what I thought of Nora's question,
or whether he wanted to know something else.

Come Christmas

It snowed again just before Christmas.
The snow got almost as high as Nora.
"Oh," she said, "what a wonderful
Christmas this will be."
I went to see if I had any mail
from New Mexico,
but I didn't.

Our grandparents' Christmas tree was up
in the living room with nothing on it yet.

It was a blue spruce our grandfather had cut
from the edge of his woods.
It looked like a green *A*.

"Grandma wants us to make it be
Christmas in here," Nora said.
"You do it," I said.
"Come on, Jack," she said.
"Grandma has ribbons,
and real bells, and even these little glass icicles."
"No," I said. I wondered whether
Mom had brought the strings
of red pepper lights from home.

Nora looked at our grandfather
the way she looks at Dad
when she wants money.
But Grandfather only smiled a little smile at her,
and went on reading the paper.

The next day, just before supper,
Grandfather came in from feeding the birds.
He didn't stop to hang up his cap and coat.
He didn't stomp the snow off on the mat.

And then we saw why.
He had three chickadees riding on his cap.

He went into the living room.
The cold was a path behind him,
and we followed in it.
He had snow on his boots and his shoulders.
But he stopped beside the Christmas tree,
waiting.

Some of the snow on his coat turned clear
and slid and tumbled down the sleeve.
Nora and I stayed in the doorway,
wondering.
Grandmother came up behind us
wiping her hands on her apron.

Soon one chickadee,
and then the other two,
flew into the tree by the window.

Still Grandfather stood there, waiting.
Then, after a long time—
    Chick-a-dee-dee-dee.
    Chick-a-dee-dee-dee.

The little birds flitted to different branches.
They sang and sang from the blue spruce tree,
as though they had come home from far away.

My grandmother opened her mouth.
She was going to say something
about the furniture
and what birds might do to it, I thought.
But she never did.

We just stood there and looked at the only tree
Grandfather had ever decorated.
A Christmas tree with live decorations
that moved and sang and looked at us.
The best Christmas tree anyone had ever seen.

When Grandfather opened his hand,
there was seed in it.
He put some on his cap.
The chickadees came to him,
like always,
like bits of metal to a magnet.

They fluttered around him,
and took their places
and the seeds.

And they all went out again
into the snow and the cold,
the little birds and Grandfather.

More birds flew around him
at the red feeder.
They chick-a-deed him.
They made me laugh.
They looked like little planes
swooping a tower.

That night, after supper and milking,
Nora and I looked out the kitchen window.
The lights from inside pushed the dark
a little way out from the house.

My sister said, "Look,"
and pointed to the icy branches
clicking on the windowpane.
"Clear Popsicles."

She made me laugh too.
She took my hands and danced around.
"Now," she said, "let's do the tree. Please?"

Grandfather came in from the barn.
He snapped his cap against his knee
and hung it by the door.
"Look," I said to him and pointed at my sister,
still fluttering around.
"She's a chickadee."

He smiled his little smile.
"Better see what she wants," he said.
So Nora and I went to decorate.

We hung up the bells and the glass icicles.
And Nora strung the ribbons
down the branches.
We both stood back to look.
"It's nice," she said.
"But not as nice
as with Grandpa's decorations."

Nothing would ever be that good.

I smiled a smile like Grandfather's.
"No," I said, "but we'll get used to it."

Den of Lions

Becky Davis

*illustrated by
Mary Ann Lumm*

*Daniel, a godly young Jew, was among the captives brought
to Babylon. He served the Lord faithfully over sixty years
and became a chief ruler in Babylon. When Darius the Mede
conquered Babylon, Daniel continued to have great influence
in the government.*

When the king made Daniel one of the chief rulers
of the land, the other presidents and princes became
jealous. "Why should this captive be a ruler over us?"
they murmured. "His position rightfully belongs to
one of us. He always interferes with our plans. Let's
find some way to get rid of him."

Every day they watched Daniel. Every day they
looked and looked to see whether they could find
something he had done wrong. But Daniel was
always wise and good and trustworthy.

So evil men gathered for a meeting. "The only way
we can find anything against him," one man said, "is
in his worship of his God." And then they made a
wicked plan.

Before long all these presidents and princes came before King Darius. They bowed and said, "O King Darius, live forever. All the chief men of the kingdom have talked together. We think it would be wise for you to make a decree to test the loyalty of all your subjects. O King, make a decree that for thirty days no one can ask any request of any god or any man except you. If he does, he shall be cast into the den of lions. Make a law, and sign it so that it cannot be changed."

The princes knew that they could catch Daniel praying to his God. But they had lied when they said that all of the chief men had talked together. Daniel, second only to the king, had not been part of the decision at all.

King Darius liked the idea of having so much power. He didn't even stop to think about Daniel. He quickly signed the decree.

Everyone in the kingdom soon heard that for a whole month they could pray to no one but the king. Daniel heard about it too. When he found out, he went up to his room, just as he had always done. He opened his windows and bowed down toward Jerusalem to pray. "O God," he prayed, "I know that the king's decree is wrong. I know that it is right for me to pray to You. I trust You to care for me as You always have. I thank You for Your protection."

But as Daniel prayed, men were watching him. The wicked princes who had made up the decree saw that he broke the law. They rubbed their hands together and said, "We have him now! He wouldn't stop praying even if his life were in danger. And it is!"

Quickly they ran to King Darius. "O King," they said, "is it not true that you signed a decree that no one could pray to anyone but you for a month?"

"That is true," King Darius replied. "And it is a law that cannot be changed."

"But," the men said triumphantly, "Daniel still prays to his God three times a day. He has not regarded the decree that you made."

The king was stunned. "Of course," he thought to himself. "Why didn't I remember that Daniel would pray to his God anyway? I never meant for him to be hurt."

The king sent the princes away. All that day he talked with his counselors and wise men, trying to find some way to rescue Daniel. But there was no way. He had signed the law himself.

At sundown the princes returned. "Your law, O King, cannot be changed," they reminded him.

King Darius knew that all too well. "Bring Daniel here," he said.

Soon gray-haired Daniel stood before the throne, knowing that he would be cast into the lions' den.

"Daniel," said King Darius, "your God whom you serve so faithfully—surely He will deliver you."

Then the servants took Daniel away and threw him into the pit. They rolled the stone over the top and sealed it so that no one could try to help Daniel escape.

King Darius couldn't eat or sleep that night. He
sent all his musicians away. He tossed and turned on
his bed, hoping that Daniel's God would deliver him.

As soon as the first light of dawn peeked through
the window, the king ran to the den of lions. Calling
his servants, he commanded them to remove the
stone. Then the king stepped to the edge and peered
into the pit.

"Oh, Daniel!" he cried, almost in tears. "Oh, Daniel,
servant of the living God, was your God able to
deliver you from the lions?"

Out of the pit came a voice. "O King, live forever."
It was the voice of Daniel! "My God sent His angel to
shut the lions' mouths. They have not hurt me."

Oh, how happy King Darius was then! "Take Daniel out of the den of lions!" he shouted to his servants.

So Daniel was brought up out of the hole without even a scratch on his body. God had protected him because Daniel believed in Him.

The princes could hardly believe that Daniel was alive. They were just about to complain when King Darius gave another command. "Throw these wicked men into the pit!" he shouted.

Was Daniel kept safe because the lions weren't hungry? No! When the princes were thrown in, the lions broke all their bones before the men even hit the bottom of the den.

Then King Darius made a new decree and sent it through all the kingdom: "In every part of my kingdom," he said, "men shall fear Daniel's God. He is the living God. He shall reign forever, and His kingdom shall never be destroyed. He works great miracles in all the earth. He is the God that delivered Daniel from the power of the lions!"

A Lamb's Tale

Gail Fitzgerald and Dawn L. Watkins
illustrated by Steve Mitchell

Mercy

Rico shifted his shoeshine
box from one hand to the
other as he struggled up
the steep slope. He stopped
a moment to rest and look back
down the mountain. Ayacucho stretched below,
a great bulk of the town half-hidden in the shadows
of the Peruvian mountains. Already lights were
blinking on in the houses. "I'm going to be late," Rico
thought, hurrying on. "But it has been a good day.
There were many, many shoes to shine."

Coins clinked in his pocket as he scrambled over a
large rock. Rico jumped down, holding the shoeshine
box carefully. When he reached the path to his house,
he began to run. Ahead of him the setting sun bathed
his adobe house in gold and outlined the reed fence.
Rico ran past the fence, shouting, "Hello, hello," to
the startled goat. He threw open the back door.
"Mama, I'm home!"

"So I can hear." Señora Perez gave Rico a hug. "I'm glad you took the shortcut up the mountain instead of taking the road. There have been many cars on the road today making dust over everything!"

"I know. Look, Mama." Rico emptied his pockets onto the table. "There were many tourists in town today. Dust makes many shoes to shine."

"Ah, Rico." His mother smiled. "Your papa will be pleased. Go wash up now, dusty one."

When Rico returned to the kitchen, cheeks red from scrubbing, his father stood in the doorway, holding something in his arms. He turned sideways to ease his burden into the house.

"Oh, the poor thing." Rico's mother put her hand to her mouth.

"It's a lamb." Rico touched the little limp head. "It's a sick lamb!"

"Wherever did you get it?" Señora Perez asked her husband.

"One of Pablo's ewes had twins. This one was the weakest, and its mother would not feed it." Señor Perez looked at Rico. "It probably won't live long."

"I'll take care of it, Papa." Rico held out his arms.

Señor Perez handed his burden to Rico. He looked at his wife.

Señora Perez shook her head. "We don't have any medicine. Neither do we have any extra milk."

"I'll give the lamb my share of the goat's milk." Rico held the lamb close. "And I'll pray to the Lord. He is the Great Shepherd, and He can make it better."

His mother's face softened. "All right, Rico."

Rico smiled, his eyes shining. "*Gracias,* Mama, Papa, *gracias!*"

It didn't take long to make a small bed of fresh-smelling straw in the corner. Rico gently laid the little lamb on the straw. Señora Perez knelt beside them, holding a bowl of milk. "I warmed it a little," she said. "She won't take cold milk."

"*Gracias,* Mama." Propping the lamb's head in his lap, Rico carefully spooned the milk into the lamb's mouth. The milk ran out the other side and dripped onto Rico's pants.

"Try this way." Rico's father took a clean cloth and twisted it at the end. He dipped the end into the warm milk and put it into the lamb's mouth. Nothing happened. Again Señor Perez dipped the cloth into the warm milk and put it into the lamb's mouth. Rico prayed silently for the lamb to take the milk. The lamb stirred. With a little whimper she began to suck the cloth.

"It worked!" Rico reached for the cloth.

"She's a long way from being well." Rico's father stood up. "But it's a beginning."

That night Rico slept on the floor close to the little lamb. He had planned to stay awake all night, but he was too tired. In the morning a weak "baa, baa" sounded in his ear. Rico's eyes blinked open.

"You are better, little lamb," he said. "*Gracias*, Lord, *gracias!*"

He cuddled the lamb in his arms, stroking its soft wool. The lamb nuzzled closer, seeking its morning meal. Rico laughed. "Warm milk is what you need. You'll eat and get well."

Though the lamb had begun to eat, it was still not strong enough to walk. Rico carried it out into the sunshine. The lamb lay in the grass as Rico hoed the potatoes. It curled up in the straw as Rico milked the goat, looking up to bleat softly when Rico was finished.

"Now, I can't carry you and the milk." The little lamb nudged his legs. "Besides, you would have your nose in the pail in no time, greedy one." Rico went to the kitchen and came back for the lamb.

"Look, Mama," Rico called. His mother opened the door. "My lamb is looking better today, don't you think?"

His mother smiled. "Yes, Rico, she does look a little better now."

"I'm going to call her Mercy!" Rico said, looking at the lamb. "That's just the name for my lamb!"

"It is?" asked Mama.

"Yes, in Psalms it says, 'Surely goodness and mercy shall follow me.' And soon I hope this little lamb will follow me on her own four feet."

"Ah," said Mama.

The lamb looked up at her with big brown eyes.

"Baa, baa." Mercy pushed against Señora Perez's hand. Rico stroked her and studied his mother's face.

"You don't think she will get well, Mama?"

"Only God knows, Rico. But you must remember that whatever happens, it is God's will."

Rico ran his fingers through the lamb's wool. "My little lamb will give us thick wool, Mama. Then you will have a new skirt, and Father and I will have new sweaters."

His mother smiled. "Now, Rico." Then she patted his head. "As seemeth good to the Lord, son, so shall it be."

Rico did not say any more.

Rico carried Mercy everywhere he went. Wherever Rico was, there was Mercy.

"You should leave her inside the fence," Señor Perez said one day. "She will never get well without more rest."

"Yes, Papa." Rico followed him across the field.

"I was just thinking," said Papa. "So many people take the road over the mountains to see the Inca ruins. The road is good for business."

"Yes, Papa?"

Señor Perez nodded. "I have been thinking of putting a stand beside the road to sell vegetables. Your mother could sell her rugs, too."

"The tourists would stop to buy them!" Rico said. "It is a good idea. And I can shine more shoes."

"Yes. Now, I want you to put Mercy into the pen with the goat," his father said. "She will be better off there."

But Mercy was not happy in the pen. She bleated and bleated. Rico went many times to pet her and offer her milk. But he always put Mercy back into the pen.

Señora Perez shook her head. "What a good friend that lamb has."

"She looks better every day," Rico said. "Yes?"

Mama sighed. "The stand is almost finished."

Rico stood and closed the gate. "Papa said he would be here every Saturday to help you at the stand." He looked at Mercy. She lay still.

His mother nodded. "If business goes well, maybe you won't have to go to Ayacucho anymore."

Goodness

The next Saturday Rico hurried down the mountain trail, eager to be at the bottom before the red sun spread out her warm blanket for the day.

"If I work hard enough today," Rico thought, "I can leave early. Then I can help Mama and Papa at the stand."

When Rico reached town, he quickly picked out the best spot and waited. Soon the streets were full of people going in and out of the stores. "Shine your shoes?" Rico called. "Shoes shined!"

Business was good. Rico shined black shoes, brown shoes, and tan shoes. There were even a few pairs of dark purple shoes and white shoes to shine. Hour after hour he worked; the thought of going home early made him forget his aching shoulders and sore fingers.

At last, Rico could work no longer. It seemed as though every muscle in his body was complaining at once. After putting away his shoeshine tools and picking up the box, he began the long walk home.

Finally he turned off onto the path leading home. He stopped at the fence to say hello to Mercy, then went into the kitchen to leave his shoeshine box. Out again, he called to the bleating Mercy, "Be good. I'll be back soon." Rico hurried down to the road.

Señor and Señora Perez looked up with surprise as Rico rounded the corner of the brightly painted stand. "Business was good in town." Rico handed his father the coins. "How is it here?"

"Good." Señora Perez showed Rico the few rugs she had left. "Many people stopped to buy vegetables. And some bought my rugs!"

"It has gone well," Rico's father agreed. "But it is time to close for the day. Rico, you can help me pack the vegetables onto the cart while your mother goes to milk the goat."

Señora Perez walked up the path to the house, counting the coins as she went. Rico and his father began to pack the vegetables onto the cart.

"There are still people on the road. Why not wait until they are gone?" Rico asked.

"The sun is beginning to go down." His father pointed toward the horizon. "You and your mother will open the stand Monday while I am at work."

Rico had lifted the last box of vegetables onto the cart when he heard a cry from the house. Señora Perez appeared on the hill, looking down at them.

"What is it?" Señor Perez called. Rico ran up the hill.

"It is Mercy," she said, and her eyes were full of tears.

"Mercy," Rico shouted. "I'm coming!"

He bolted past his mother, but his father stopped him. "Wait, Rico."

Rico looked back at his father.

Just then a big car pulled in beside the stand.

"*Buenos días,*" a man called with an American accent.

Señor Perez looked toward the car and back at his son. Then he called to the man, "I am sorry, señor, but my stand is closed."

"But I just want to buy a rug," the man called back.

"I am again sorry, señor, but my son's lamb is sick, and we have to go."

"Wait," the man said. He got out of the car. "I'm a vet—an animal doctor. Let me come help." He waited by the car.

Rico's heart raced. His father said at last, "*Gracias,* señor."

The man came up the hill and then followed them to the pen. Mercy lay on her side, breathing heavily.

"Will she be all right, Papa?"

"I don't know, Rico." Señor Perez knelt in the dust beside him.

Señora Perez wiped her eyes with her apron and put her arm around Rico's shoulders.

The American checked the little lamb. Then he looked up at Rico's father and shook his head. "I'm afraid that even if I had all my medicine and equipment, I would not be able to help."

Rico stood up. "But the Lord can heal her." He rubbed at his eyes with the back of his hand. "He can do it. I know it!"

"Yes, He can, Rico." Señor Perez lifted Rico's chin with his hand. "But He might choose not to." Rico looked into his father's face. Tears ran down his neck and onto his shirt. "I'm sorry, Son." Señor Perez pulled Rico to him. "Why don't you go to the house? I'll take care of the lamb."

Rico looked up at his father. He wiped the tears from his face. "I want to stay and take care of her, Papa." He dried his hands on his pants.

The vet still stroked the lamb's head. The breathing was slower now. In only a little time, it stopped. Rico caught a sob in his throat.

"I have seen many sick lambs," the vet said. "And I think it would help you to know that this one would never have been strong and well. It was a mercy that she died so peacefully."

Rico looked at his father. "A mercy," he repeated.

A week later Señora Perez looked out the window. "Rico," she said, "there is a man coming up the hill. Run and see if he wants to buy something. I will come out soon."

Rico went out. He went past the goat's pen. It still hurt him to look into the pen and not see Mercy.

"Hurry, Rico," his mother called. "Do not make the man walk all the way up the hill."

Rico went faster. Then he saw that the man was the vet who had stopped only the week before.

"Señor," he said. "*Buenos días.*"

"Hello," said the man. "I was wondering—"

Señora Perez now joined them. "Señor," she said, "we are pleased to see you again."

"Señora," he said, "I would like to make a trade."

"Señor?"

"My wife wants another fine rug from your stand. And I was hoping that you could take in exchange for it a little lamb I helped deliver a few days ago. It is fine and healthy, but the mother died."

Rico stared at the man. Could it possibly be true, this news that he was hearing?

The man went on. "I could see that your son was a good caretaker when I was here before, and I thought of him. If you think it would be all right, that is."

Señora Perez swallowed and then nodded. "*Gracias,* señor," she barely whispered.

Rico nearly galloped to the car to see the lamb.

"Will you give him a name?" the vet asked.

Rico paused. Then he said with a great big smile, "This one I will call Goodness."

Sunning

James S. Tippett / illustrated by Johanna Berg

Old Dog lay in the summer sun
Much too lazy to rise and run.
He flapped an ear
At a buzzing fly.
He winked a half opened
Sleepy eye.
He scratched himself
On an itching spot,
As he dozed on the porch
Where the sun is hot.
He whimpered a bit
From force of habit
While he lazily dreamed
Of chasing a rabbit.
But Old Dog happily lay in the sun
Much too lazy to rise and run.

A Curtain of Spun Silver

(based on a true story)

Karen Wilt
illustrated by Mary Ann Lumm

Mr. Havers bowed to pray in the rustic chapel. The men, women, and children knelt on the rough wooden floor and joined him.

They prayed for Archbishop Sheldon, who persecuted the little church and had tried to imprison Mr. Havers. They prayed for the families of the ten men who had been arrested and might be put to death. Finally, they thanked God for His loving protection and care and for the salvation He gave in Christ Jesus.

Mr. Havers hummed the closing hymn thoughtfully as the congregation rose to leave.

Two strong men slowly opened the door of the church. They crossed the creek just below the church and searched for soldiers who might be hiding nearby. At last they motioned for the others to come. Silently the congregation hurried to their cottages in the nearby villages.

At home Mr. Havers opened his Bible and started to study. Someone knocked loudly at the door. Mr. Havers rose and opened the peephole. A young boy stood gasping for breath, his cheeks bright red and fear in his eyes.

"What troubleth thee?" Mr. Havers asked, lifting the latch.

"The men who work for Archbishop Sheldon just rode through the village. They seek thy life." The boy held his side. "Flee, Mr. Havers. They are hardhearted and will not let you live to be tried fairly."

Mr. Havers glanced toward the village. A cloud of dust rose above the thatched roofs.

"See, their horses approach even now," the boy said. "Oh, please flee, Mr. Havers." The boy turned and raced to the gate.

"Trust God," Mr. Havers called in his strong, deep voice. "He shall protect us both."

He slipped his Bible into his inside pocket, closed the door behind him, and dashed into the woods. Hooves thundered past him on the road. Out of sight, he ran toward the mill. As he crossed an open field, he heard a cry go up from the far road. The horsemen had reached the empty house.

Mr. Havers dared run no farther. Finding the house empty, the men would search the woods and fields.

He slipped into a malt house, searching for a place to hide. Only an empty kiln seemed big enough to crawl inside. Mr. Havers slid as far as possible into the dark shadows, but the sunlight poured in through an open window and lit up the doorway of the kiln.

As he lay curled up on the brick floor, panting for breath, a spider dropped across the doorway, trailing a long thread behind her. Back and forth the spider swung, attaching her silk to the top and sides in wider and wider circles.

The long strands soon covered the door of the kiln in a beautiful design. The web glistened like spun silver in the light from the window.

Suddenly the door of the malt house burst open. Heavy boots tramped across the floor. Mr. Havers held his breath. He had forgotten he was hiding as he watched the spider.

"He must be in here. I'll break his head when I catch him, I will," a gruff voice said.

The steps moved closer to the kiln. "It's no use to look in there. The old villain can never be there. Look at that spider's web. He could never have gotten in there without breaking it."

"Come on, then. He must have escaped through the woods," the first voice said.

The door closed. Mr. Havers waited until all was quiet. "A curtain of spun silver to hide me," he murmured, slipping through the spider web and escaping to safety. He paused briefly to thank the Lord for His protection brought about by a little spider and her web.

The Web Weavers

Wendy M. Harris

Spiders are famous for their webs, but not all kinds of spiders make webs. All spiders do make silk though. Most spiders have about six tiny tubes called spinnerets on their abdomens. Each tiny tube, or spinneret, makes a different kind of thread. Some threads are sticky. Some threads are nonsticky. The spider uses its feet to pull the thread out of the spinnerets.

Have you ever wondered how a spider dashes up and down its sticky web and does not get stuck like insects do? God gave the spider a special oil on its claws. The oil keeps the spider from sticking to the silky threads of the web.

To begin weaving a web, the spider perches somewhere and pulls out a thread of sticky silk. The length of silk flutters in the breeze until it sticks to something solid nearby. Then the spider anchors the other end of the silk thread. That makes a bridge. The spider scrambles back and forth across the bridge several times. Each time he lays down more strands of silk to strengthen the bridge.

Next the spider adds a frame of nonsticky silk lines and cables to the bridge. The lines and cables are attached to other nearby objects, like twigs and leaves. This frame looks a little like a wheel with spokes that meet in the center.

Once the lines are in place, the little weaver begins in the center of the frame and spins a nonsticky thread. He goes around and around the cables in a larger and larger spiral. This middle area is now a small platform that the spider sits on while eating a meal. Some spiders later rest on their platforms while waiting for insects to be trapped in the web.

The rest of the spider's trap is formed by a second, larger spiral. Using sticky silk, the spider spins a thread farther out on the web. Around and around circles the spider again. This time he is weaving closer and closer toward the platform in the middle. When the spider finishes the sticky spiral, its web is complete. It can take less than an hour to weave a web.

Now the spider prepares for a meal! It attaches a nonsticky thread to the web's center. Then it scurries away to hide. This last thread is a signal thread. The spider holds on to the other end of the thread and waits in its hiding place for the signal.

If an insect is trapped in the web, the spider may not see it. But the signal thread picks up the vibrations of any movement. This thread lets the spider feel the struggles of a bug trying to get free. Then the spider races across the lines to wrap up its victim with more silk.

Many people do not like to look at spiders or to think about them. You may think that spiders are ugly. But God created these web weavers to be our helpers. Their webs catch grasshoppers and locusts that harm crops. Their webs also catch flies and mosquitoes that bother us and carry diseases. The next time you see a web, remember all that spiders do for us. God made them to be more than just web weavers.

Under the Tent of the Sky

*Rowena
Bastin Bennett*

illustrated by Johanna Berg

The wind cracked his whip,
The storm flashed a gun,
And the animal-clouds marched one by one
Under the tent of the sky.

There were elephants, blue,
And shaggy white bears,
And dozens and dozens of prancing gray mares
With their beautiful heads held high.

There were soft-footed panthers
And ostriches, fluffy,
And a great hippopotamus, purple and puffy,
Who wallowed in mud-colored mist.

There were small curly dogs
And camels with humps
And a wrinkled rhinoceros, all over bumps,
With a horn as big as your fist.

There was even a lion
Bedecked with a mane
Who growled so loud that he turned into rain
And tumbled to earth with a sigh.

The wind cracked his whip
And out came the sun
And the animal-clouds passed one by one
Out of the tent of the sky.

What About Dolphins?

Becky Davis and Eileen M. Berry

The dolphin isn't an ordinary fish. In fact, the dolphin isn't a fish at all—it's a mammal. That means it has to breathe air just the way you and I do. The dolphin's "nose" is on top of its head, like a whale's. It can close its "nose" while it swims underwater, but it has to get back to the surface every few minutes to take another breath.

Dolphins almost always travel in groups called schools. Not only do they play games together—games like catch and tag—but they also help take care of each other. If a dolphin is hurt and can't get to the surface of the water to breathe, another dolphin will push it up to the surface and hold it there. The members of the school also protect each other from enemies, such as sharks.

If a shark sees a baby dolphin, it will often try to kill it. The baby dolphin looks like a good meal for the shark until all the dolphin family attacks. With their powerful snouts they ram the shark's side again and again. Dolphins can usually kill an attacking shark.

Why is all this important to man? Even though dolphins can kill a shark, they won't attack people, even the people who capture or hurt them. Why not? No one knows. But there are even stories of dolphins' saving the lives of drowning swimmers. There is no other wild animal that is as friendly to man as the dolphin.

This friendliness aroused people's interest in finding out more about dolphins. In 1938, the first of many ocean theme parks opened with dolphins as a main attraction! Squeaking and rasping, these friendly creatures stuck their heads out of the water and tossed seashells to the spectators. If someone threw a ball into their tank, the dolphins threw it back. The people, enjoying the dolphins' playfulness, went back again and again just to see the dolphins.

Soon people found that these clever creatures could do a few tricks on their own. Trainers found ways to teach dolphins new and more complicated tricks. Some dolphins learned to play basketball, rise up on their tails in the water, and jump up twenty feet to ring a bell. The dolphins seemed to love to learn and to be with the people who taught them.

Before long, scientists became interested in dolphins. By testing these creatures, they found dolphins to be one of the most intelligent kinds of animals on earth. Scientists learned that the dolphin could move very fast underwater, much faster than ships. Scientists also learned that the dolphin could come up from deep water quickly without getting sick the way divers do. Finally, they found that a dolphin could find objects underwater very easily

with a system called *sonar*.

A dolphin's sonar helps him "see" objects with his ears, even in the muddiest water. By making clicking noises and listening to the echoes, he can tell how far away an object is, how big it is, and even what kind of material it is made of. A sonar device on one of our ships isn't nearly as good as a dolphin's. The dolphin can tell the difference between two different kinds of little fish, but with our sonar, men sometimes can't tell the difference between a ship and a whale! Scientists are working hard to learn all that they can from this marvelous system the Lord gave to dolphins.

Dolphins are now being used in other kinds of experiments too. Scientists are studying the way dolphins seem to be able to communicate with each other. Some medical researchers use dolphins to work with people who have physical or emotional problems. The United States Navy is experimenting with ways to use dolphins to retrieve objects and to hunt for mines in the oceans.

In recent years, some areas of the world have passed laws to try to keep dolphins from being killed. Dolphins and tuna often swim together, and dolphins are easily tangled in tuna fishermen's nets and drowned. Some dolphins die when toxic waste is dumped into the oceans. It is hoped that the new laws will help protect the dolphin from these dangers.

God has created the world and its creatures for our enjoyment and use. But He has also given us the responsibility of caring for His creation. With a little care, we will be able to enjoy dolphins for many years to come.

Fremont's Frog Farm

Gail Fitzgerald
and Susan W. Young

illustrated by Bruce Day

A Better Way Than Lemonade

Monty looked at his watch—five o'clock.
He looked at the three piles of coins in front of him
and sighed. The big pile of coins went to his mother
for lemons and sugar. The middle-sized pile of coins
went to his father for paper cups. And the small pile
was his. He sighed again. One dollar and twenty-three
cents wasn't nearly enough to buy the baseball mitt
in Mr. White's window. He had to find a better way
to earn money.

Monty poured himself the last cup of lemonade.
Then he went over to the lilac bush in front of the
house and pulled out the paper the newsboy had
thrown there. He sipped the lemonade and flipped
page after page.

"Hey, look at that! A restaurant that serves frog legs."
Monty read the ad out loud. "Fried frog legs—delicious,
delectable, and tasty. Hmm." He turned the page.

"Fremont! Fremont Brown!" Mom stood at the back
door. "Supper's ready."

Monty stuffed the paper into his back pocket. "Coming, Mom." With quick strokes he brushed the grass off his jeans. Suddenly he jerked the paper out of his pocket. "That's it!" He flipped open the paper. "I can go into business selling frogs!"

The next morning, Monty woke before it was light and slipped into his clothes. He tiptoed down the stairs and let himself out the kitchen door without a sound. He loaded his fishing net, his dad's high-powered flashlight, and an old burlap sack into his bike basket. He turned his bike down the lane to the pond.

At the pond, Monty waded out into the water and turned back to face the bank. He shone the flashlight carefully along the edge of the water, searching for frogs.

"Come out, come out, wherever you are." The mud sucked at his tennis shoes. "I know you're out there. And I'm going to find you."

Suddenly the light shone into the bulging eyes of a slick green frog. Blinded by the light, the frog did not move a muscle, and with one quick move Monty scooped him up in the net. "Gotcha." Monty dumped the frog into the burlap sack tied to his belt. "That's one."

He swung the flashlight to the right. "Aha!" The net went down and came up full of frog. "Wow, you're a big one. Lots of meat on those legs. Mr. Frog, you're going to help me buy a baseball glove. Now all I have to do is find your friends and relatives, and I'll really be in business." Monty dumped him into the bag and closed the top quickly so the first frog could not jump out.

For the next two hours, Monty sloshed through the water along the muddy bank, blinding frogs with the flashlight and catching them in his net. At last, with his arms aching and his pantlegs dripping, Monty pedaled off toward the house. The frogs inside the bag bumped and thumped in the bike basket. "Twenty-five frogs and just two hours' work." Monty said the words into the wind as he headed for home. "I think this is my best plan yet."

The sun had just hit the back porch when Monty squished up the back steps. The heavy burlap bag bumped against his leg.

The door opened. Monty's mother's eyes traveled up from the squishing sneakers, to the dripping pants, and finally to the burlap bag thumping and jumping in his hands. "Fremont Preston Brown, where have you been?" She always used his full name when he was late for meals. "And what do you have in there?" She smiled just a little as she stepped out onto the porch.

"Frogs." Monty shifted the bag to his other hand. Who would have thought that twenty-five frogs could be so heavy?

"Frogs! Oh, Mom, you're not going to let him bring them in the house, are you?" complained thirteen-year-old Patti Ann, who had joined them on the porch. Monty looked at her from under his lowered eyebrows.

Just then Dad stepped out onto the porch. "What's all the commotion about?"

Monty set the bag on the ground and rubbed his muddy hands against his muddy shirt. If he could make Dad understand, then he was home free. "Well, Dad, I got up early and went down to the pond and this is why I went." Monty pointed to the bag.

"It's full of frogs." Patti Ann wrinkled her nose.

Monty ignored her. "You see, Dad, I just can't make enough money selling lemonade, so I've decided to raise frogs and sell them to the Country Kitchen for the most delicious, delectable, and tasty treat they've ever had on their menu. I saw an ad in the paper for some restaurant that serves frog legs. That's what gave me the idea." A frown was starting at the corners of Dad's mouth. Little furrows were forming between his eyebrows. Monty hurried on. "So I went down to the pond this morning to get some frogs. There were hundreds of them. At least a year's supply. Please, Dad, let me try this. I think it will work."

"How many frogs did you catch this morning?" Dad looked down at the bag bouncing and bulging on the porch.

"Twenty-five."

"Twenty-five frogs!" Mom and Patti Ann said at the same time.

"And just where do you plan to keep these twenty-five frogs, Son?" The furrows between Dad's eyebrows were getting deeper.

"In my room."

"Dad, you can't let him do that." Patti Ann threw a glance at Monty. "You can't let him bring those smelly old frogs into the house."

"He's not planning to keep them in *your* room, Patti Ann." The furrows were gone from between Dad's eyebrows. "Are you, Monty?"

"Oh, no, sir. They'll stay in my room safe and sound. Besides, Patti Ann, you got to keep goldfish in your room once."

"That's not the same thing, and you know it." Patti Ann crossed her arms and stuck out her lower lip.

"Now, Patti Ann, we'll have none of that. Besides, this may be a great learning experience for Monty." Dad rubbed his chin. Monty knew he always did that when he was thinking. "I once had a friend who raised mice in his bedroom." Monty's mom just shook her head and smiled. "Today he's a successful scientist. Who knows where this venture might take you." Dad stopped rubbing his chin. "All right, Son, you may keep the frogs in your own room in Patti Ann's old aquarium, but just until they are sold. They are your responsibility, and I'd better not find them in my shoes."

"Thanks, Dad. I'll sell them just as soon as I can, I promise." Monty picked up the bag and headed in the door.

"Not so fast, young man." Mom blocked the way. Her arms were folded, but her eyes were smiling. "Take those muddy shoes off out here and hose the mud off your pants. When you're dry, you may come in. You can have the frogs in the house, but please don't leave mud on my carpets." Monty knew Mom wanted to keep those frogs outside as long as possible.

His pants were not completely dry when Monty disappeared upstairs, but at least they weren't dripping. The bag went thump, thump, thump against his leg at his every step.

The old aquarium that had held Patti Ann's fish wasn't quite big enough to hold twenty-five frogs, so Monty put in as many as he could and then went to find something, anything that would hold a frog. Soon he had every bucket, pan, and jar he could find. There was hardly room to walk.

"Son," Dad said the next morning, stifling a yawn. "Those frogs kept me awake all night!"

Monty squirmed in his seat. "They were kind of noisy, weren't they? But I got used to them after a while."

"Well, I didn't!" Patti Ann plopped down into her chair.

"You are planning to sell them, aren't you?" Mom covered a yawn.

"I'm going to try to sell them. I'm not sure they'll all be gone today."

"The sooner the better." And by the way Dad raised his bushy eyebrows and squared his jaw, Monty knew he meant business.

The Catch of the Day

Later that morning Monty paused in front of the Country Kitchen and studied his reflection in the big glass window. Balancing a large box in one hand, he tucked in his shirt with the other and then pushed open the door.

Thump, thump, thump. Monty clutched the box tightly as he wound his way among the tables of chattering people to the counter at the back. He climbed up onto a stool and waited until Mr. Murphy finished serving a stranger.

"Howdy, Mr. Murphy. I've heard that you've got the best restaurant in town."

Mr. Murphy laughed. "Thanks, Monty. I've got the only restaurant in town."

Monty was glad to see Mr. Murphy in good humor. He plunged into his speech. "Would you like to buy some frogs for your restaurant? Frog legs are delicious, delectable, and tasty. The frogs only cost twenty cents apiece. I have twenty-five with me today and can catch plenty more. If you want them, I can bring them right to your door every week. The fresher the better, you know."

Mr. Murphy shook his head. "I'm sorry, Monty, it just wouldn't work. Serving frog legs is a great idea and folks might like them, but my wife's the cook around here, and she hates frogs."

Monty looked down and kicked his toe against the counter.

"I'm sorry, kid." Mr. Murphy rubbed the counter with his cloth. "I'm sure you've got nice frogs. They sound lively enough. Maybe you could advertise in the paper. There are bound to be restaurants in other towns that would *jump* at a chance to sell frog legs." Mr. Murphy tipped back his head and laughed at his own joke.

"I guess I'll have to give it a try." Monty picked up his box. "Thanks anyway, Mr. Murphy."

"Excuse me, Son." A stranger at the counter tapped Monty's shoulder. "May I take a look at your frogs?"

"Sure, Mister. You want to buy some frogs?" Monty set the box on the counter and pried open one corner of the top. The stranger bent over to look.

Thump, thump, thump. All of the frogs jumped at once for the small corner of light.

Backward fell the stranger, up into the air went the box, and out came the frogs.

"Oh, no!" yelled Mr. Murphy, waving his towel in the air.

"I'll get them! I'll get them!" shouted Monty, diving under tables and scrambling over chairs.

Half an hour later Monty backed out the door. The box went thump, thump, thump in his hands. Mr. Murphy was still busy trying to get his customers reseated, and the stranger was on his hands and knees looking for the last frog.

A few days later Monty paced back and forth in front of the house. Sometimes he ran to the gate and looked down the street. But it was while he was getting a drink of water in the house that the *Shelbyville News* arrived. Thud!

Monty made a dive under the porch and pulled out the paper. With his heart pounding, he turned to the last page.

"Here it is!" he yelled, running inside and waving the paper. "Here's my ad!" He pointed to the tiny three-line ad. Mom and Patti Ann crowded around to see.

> Frogs for sale. Will make delicious, delectable, and tasty frog legs. 5 frogs for $1.00. Call 235-2335.

Monty laid the paper on the counter. "The phone will start ringing off the hook any minute now."

Mom smiled and patted Monty's shoulder. "I hope so, Monty, I hope so."

Monty sat down on the chair next to the phone with pencil and paper in his hands. "I'll just sit right here and take orders."

By dinner time Monty had used up all his paper.

"Those are good pictures, Son," Dad said. "But how many orders did you get?"

"None." Monty shook his head. "Not a single one."

"Too bad Mr. Murphy down at the Country Kitchen wouldn't buy your frogs." Patti Ann leaned against the counter beside him.

"Yeah, it sure *is*." Monty flipped the pad of paper shut and put down the pencil. "Now I have to figure out what else frogs are good for." Monty glanced over at the paper. The headline caught his eye.

Scientists Look for Nonchemical Means to Kill Flies

"We don't have any flies around our house, that's for sure." A half grin appeared on Monty's face; then it erupted into a full-blown shout. "That's it! I'll sell my frogs to the neighbors as flycatchers!"

It's Happened Before

Monty hurried down the street, his heart thumping double time to the thump, thump, thump of the frogs in the box.

"This is it," he thought as he knocked on the first door. "I've found a way to sell hundreds and thousands of frogs—or at least twenty-four."

"Yes?" The lady had her purse and keys in her hand.

"I see you are on your way out, Ma'am, but I wonder if I could interest you in a frog or two to catch your flies?"

"I don't catch flies. I swat them. Now if you'll excuse me . . ."

Monty escaped to the next house with the echo of the slammed door sounding in his ears.

"Howdy, Grandma Bell." He climbed the porch step at the next house. "Nice day, isn't it?" Monty eyed the fly swatter in her hand.

"It would be without these pesky flies."

Smack! The fly swatter fell just short of a huge black fly. Her rocking chair squeaked as she reached to swat at another one. "Seems like they know I can't move around to get them. They stay just out of my reach."

"I've got just the thing you need." Monty groped around in his box and pulled out a plump green frog. "This big guy will catch all your flies."

"Well, looky there." Grandma peered over her glasses.

"I'm selling frogs as fly catchers," said Monty, "to earn money to buy a new mitt."

"Well, every boy needs a good baseball mitt. I'll take two of those frogs, Monty."

"Thanks, Grandma Bell! If you ever need any more, just give me a call." Monty put the coins in his pocket, picked up his thumping box, and went whistling down the street.

Four hours later Monty limped into his yard, the blisters on his feet throbbing with every step.

"Fremont, is that you?" Mom called from the kitchen. "It's five o'clock. Company will be here for dinner in just a few minutes. Go clean up quickly."

Monty put his box down, limped upstairs to his room, and emptied his pockets.

"Ten, twenty, thirty . . ." Monty counted his dimes, dividing them into piles. "One dollar goes to Dad for the newspaper ad. Fifty cents belongs to Mom for frog food. And the rest is mine." Monty sighed. "One dollar and seventy cents. I'll never get that new mitt in Mr. White's window." He ran his fingers through his hair and counted the frogs left in the containers. "Five frogs left to sell and I've been to every house in town. Now what am I going to do?"

B-r-r-ing. Monty could tell by the excited hellos that company had arrived. He pulled on a clean shirt.

"Monty! There's a frog under the table!" Patti Ann never was one to announce things quietly.

"How in the world did that happen?" Monty quickly checked the covers on the frog containers. The container nearest the door was knocked on its side and the one and only frog that had lived there was gone. "Great, I must have knocked the lid off when I came in. Mom'll never forgive me for this one and with company here for supper, too." Monty dashed down the stairs, past the company, and into the dining room. Patti Ann, standing with one hand on her hip, was pointing under the table.

"I'll get it! I'll get it!" He dived under the table.

Laughter came from the hall where the company stood. "Seems to me I've seen this happen before!"

Monty's ears burned. He had heard that voice before! He backed out from under the table, clutching the frog in his left hand. There in the dining room stood the stranger from the Country Kitchen.

"Monty," Dad said, "I'd like you to meet an old friend of mine, Mr. Bailey."

The stranger, Mr. Bailey, laughed again and slapped Monty on the back. "That's a fine looking frog you've got there, young man. Looks a lot like the one I finally caught under a table at the Country Kitchen. He can really jump."

"Thank you, sir." Monty said over his shoulder as he ran up the stairs. He could tell by the look on his mother's face this was no time for small talk.

Supper that night was *not* frog legs, but the conversation kept coming back to the subject of frogs. Monty told Mr. Bailey how he had been trying to sell frogs, first for frog legs and then for fly catchers. Mr. Bailey seemed very interested and asked Monty question after question.

"John," Monty's dad said finally. "What makes you so interested in frogs all of a sudden? Have you gone into the restaurant business?"

Mr. Bailey leaned back in his chair and laughed. "No, I'm not in the business of selling frog legs. Right now I'm interested in frog legs for a different reason. I need frog legs that can jump far and fast. I need frogs that can race."

"Frog racing?" Monty leaned so far forward that he tipped over his water glass. He caught it just in time. He heard his mom catch her breath as the water slid back down in the glass.

"Yes, frog racing." Mr. Bailey leaned toward Monty. "Every year at the County Fair we sponsor a huge frog race. The more frogs the better. Some folks bring their own, but most folks just buy one after they get there."

"They BUY them?" Now Monty was on his feet. "They BUY frogs? Can just anybody sell them?"

"Well, now there's a catch there. They generally buy them from us."

"Oh." Monty sat back down with a thump.

"Now don't give up so easy, Son. We have to buy them from someone."

"Would you buy them from me?"

"I think we might be able to do some business. How many do you have?"

"How many do you need? I've got six right now. But don't worry—I can catch more; there are plenty more where those came from."

"I'll take as many as you can get for me."

"Mr. Bailey, I'll get you the biggest, slickest, greenest frogs you have ever seen. You'll never have to go anywhere else. All the frogs you need will be right here at Fremont's Frog Farm."

"Fremont's Frog Farm!" Dad nearly choked on his coffee. Mom put her fork down with a clank. And Patti Ann covered her face with her napkin.

When Mr. Bailey left that night, he handed Monty some money. "My man will be by tomorrow to get your frogs. I'll take the six frogs you have and as many more as you can catch before my man gets here at ten. He'll pay you for the others then." Mr. Bailey shook Monty's hand.

"Yes, sir!" Monty grinned and held up the money. "Looks like I'll be giving Mr. White some business after all."

The Greedy Dog

Karen Wilt / illustrated by Justin Gerard

One day a burly brown dog bounded through town, carrying a juicy hunk of meat. As he ran over the wooden bridge that lay across the river leading home, the dog glanced into the water. On the surface of the river he saw a stout brown dog with a piece of meat hanging from its mouth. The burly brown dog bristled. The other dog bristled. He growled deep in his throat. The other dog stood silent as stone.

"Give me your meat!" the burly brown dog snarled. But as he opened his mouth to bark, his meat fell with a splash, making the reflection of himself ripple into little waves that raced to the shore. The meat disappeared into the murky depths, and all that the burly brown dog could do was bark at his own reflection.

M o r a l :
Greediness may cause one
to lose everything.

A. A. Milne

illustrated by Tim Banks

Forgiven

I found a little beetle, so that Beetle was his name,

And I called him Alexander and he answered just
the same.

I put him in a match-box, and I kept him
all the day . . .

And Nanny let my beetle out—

     Yes, Nanny let my beetle out—

     She went and let my beetle out—

     And Beetle ran away.

She said she didn't mean it, and I never said she did,

She said she wanted matches and she just took
off the lid,

She said that she was sorry, but it's difficult to catch

An excited sort of beetle you've mistaken for a match.

302

She said that she was sorry, and I really mustn't mind,

As there's lots and lots of beetles which she's certain
we could find,

If we looked about the garden for the holes where
beetles hid—

And we'd get another match-box and write BEETLE
on the lid.

We went to all the places which a beetle might
be near,

And we made the sort of noises which a beetle
likes to hear,

And I saw a kind of something, and I gave a sort
of shout:

"A beetle-house and Alexander Beetle coming out!"

It was Alexander Beetle I'm as certain as can be

And he had a sort of look as if he thought it must
    be ME,

And he had a sort of look as if he thought he ought
    to say:

"I'm very, very sorry that I tried to run away."

And Nanny's very sorry too for you-know-what-
    she-did,

And she's writing ALEXANDER very blackly
    on the lid.

So Nan and Me are friends, because it's difficult
    to catch

An excited Alexander you've mistaken for a match.

A Gift for Uncle Tom

*Gail Fitzgerald
and Susan W. Young*

illustrated by Johanna Berg

It seems as if everyone in Toby Johnson's house is doing something important to get ready for Uncle Tom's visit. Everyone, that is, except Toby. Toby's efforts to help lead only to trouble and more trouble.

The Big Catch

Toby ran up a few steps, turned around, and took a flying leap. As he jumped, he threw his rag at the chandelier hanging from the fourteen-foot ceiling.

"Mercy! Mercy!" Liza had just come around the corner with her arms full. Up into the air flew blankets, sheets, and pillows. Down on the floor tumbled the servant and the nine-year-old boy.

Toby sneezed. "Ah-choo!" Duck feathers from a torn pillow floated through the air. "Ah-choo! Ah-choo!"

"Tobias Lee Johnson! What is going on here?" Mother's voice was muffled by the blankets. Her long skirts swished angrily. He lifted one corner of the blue blanket draped over his head and peeped out. His mother stood in the doorway with her hands on her hips, the lace on her cap bouncing up and down.

"Get out from under those blankets," Mother ordered. She pulled back the piles of bedding.

Toby scrambled out and gathered up blankets, sheets, and pillows. "Ah-choo! Ah-choo! Ah-choo!"

Mother helped Liza to her feet. "Never mind the bedding, Toby."

Toby dropped his armful to the floor, sending up another shower of feathers.

"What *were* you doing?" Mother fanned the feathers from in front of her face.

"I was just trying to help." Toby looked at Mother's face and figured he had better talk quickly. "I heard you say that the chandelier needed dusting, and I couldn't reach it by standing on a chair, so I thought I could knock the dust off with my rag."

Mother shook her head. Liza turned her back to stifle a laugh. "Toby, Toby, sometimes you are too helpful. Impulsive, I think your father would say. Well, thank you for your help, but run along. There's too much to do before your Uncle Tom arrives this afternoon. You'll just have to spend the morning outside." She pointed to the door. "Now go, and make sure you're back for the special church meeting. You know Uncle Tom is going to be the preacher."

Under protest Toby backed out the door. He wandered around to the back of the large brick house. It seemed as though everyone was getting ready for Uncle Tom's arrival—everyone, that is, except him. Mary was baking bread in the kitchen; Buck was almost finished polishing the carriage; and Benjamin had the horses looking sleek and shiny. It didn't matter where Toby offered his help; he was either too little, too late, or just plain in the way.

"I think I'll take a walk," Toby said as he looked around, but everyone seemed too busy to notice him. Closing the front gate behind him, Toby started down the cobblestone street. He slid his hands into his pockets.

"Ouch!" He pulled his right hand back out again with a jerk. A fishing hook came with it, followed by ten feet of twisted string. Toby gingerly unhooked his finger and then slowly wound the string around the hook. Before he finished, he came up with a plan.

"Uncle Tom loves fresh fish." Toby turned in the direction of the river. "I'll catch him the biggest and best one he ever ate!"

Down King Street, around the corner onto Milk Street, past the butcher shop, the silversmith's, and the blacksmith's he hurried. At the baker's shop, Toby slowed down. The freshly iced hot cross buns in the window looked tempting. Toby disappeared into the shop and was back out in a moment. He ate one bun in a few quick bites and stuffed the other into his jacket pocket. Fishing just might be hard work!

At the river Toby dug around in the dirt until he found some fat worms. They were squishy too, he discovered as he tried to get a worm rather than his finger on the hook.

"Catch one for Uncle Tom," he whispered as he threw the hook with the fat worm into the water.

Nothing happened. Toby jiggled the line. He pulled a little of the line out of the water. He sighed. The only ripples on the water came from his line. He settled back to wait. For a long time Toby stared at the lacy pattern the leaves made overhead, thinking about Uncle Tom's visits. Working hard as a circuit-riding preacher, Uncle Tom usually held several special meetings at the church. Always, however, he managed to spend a little time alone with Toby. One time Uncle Tom took him to the fair. Another time they went fishing below the mill. And . . .

Toby sat up and looked at the water. Not even a nibble! Pulling the line out of the water, he baited his hook with a fatter worm. This time his line plopped right near a sunken log. Toby pulled the line up just a little. Something pulled back!

Either the fish that grabbed the fat worm was terribly strong, or the river's edge was awfully slippery. Toby found himself sliding toward the cold water.

Mud spattered and water sprayed as Toby's heels caught on a tree root. His downward slide stopped just in time. With a "heave-ho!" Toby yanked the string. The fish soared out of the water and landed on the bank behind him. Flipping and flopping, it slid down the muddy bank.

"Oh, no you don't!" With a lunge Toby fell on top of the fish. Triumphantly he staggered to his feet, the fish in his arms and a grin on his face. "Wait until Uncle Tom sees this one!"

311

On the Way Home

It seemed as though Toby's feet barely touched the ground as he headed back home carrying Uncle Tom's fish. He was halfway through the town when he heard a sound behind him.

Toby turned his head. One black cat, two gray cats, and three little yellow kittens with their noses in the air were heading toward him like boys after their mother's freshly baked bread. Toby wrapped his arms more tightly around the fish.

"Go home!" he yelled, stamping his foot. The cats came closer.

"Shoo! Get away from here!"

The big black cat rubbed against Toby's legs while the gray cats mewed pitifully. They seemed to be terribly hungry. Toby pushed them away with his foot. More cats joined them.

Toby ran. Uncle Tom's fish slipped from his grasp and slithered down the front of his jacket. Toby grabbed desperately, catching hold of its tail. A gray

cat leaped for the fish and caught its sharp claws on the edge of Toby's jacket.

Clasping the fish as tightly as he could, Toby gave a hard jerk on his jacket. There was a ripping sound as the cat fell to the road. He looked down. His pocket dangled by one corner. His hot cross bun lay icing side down in the dirt. The cats pounced on the bun, battling for the food. Toby ran down the road, not daring to look back.

Ding, dong. Ding, dong.

Toby stopped short. The church bells—he had forgotten all about Uncle Tom's meeting! What was he going to do with the fish? He didn't dare to be late for the meeting!

Toby glanced around. Outside the printer's shop lay a pile of old newspapers. Toby quickly wrapped up his fish. Then he unbuttoned his muddy jacket, laid the fish against his chest, and buttoned his jacket again. The jacket fit so snugly that the fish couldn't possibly slip out.

Breathing a sigh of relief, Toby raced for the church. Just as the bells stopped pealing, Toby slipped inside and sat down in the last pew. The newspaper crinkled and crunched.

Toby tried to sit very still. It was awfully hot! As he moved to a more comfortable position, the papers crunched loudly.

The boy next to Toby leaned over and whispered, "Whatcha got in there, Toby?"

"Nothing."

The boy raised his eyebrows and gave Toby a dig with his elbow. "Sure you do. What is it?"

A man tapped the boys on the shoulders. "Shhh!"

By this time Toby could feel the dampness of the fish through the newspaper. He fanned himself, then sniffed. "Oh, no," he groaned to himself. "It's starting to smell!"

Uncle Tom got up to speak, but Toby didn't hear a word he said. The boy next to Toby began to giggle. Then Toby saw Mrs. Tarby's nose begin to twitch and the feathers on her hat begin to bob. She leaned over and whispered something to Mrs. Morgan. Mrs. Morgan sniffed the air, nodded, and leaned over to whisper to her oldest daughter. Up and down the pews closest to Toby, people whispered and sniffed. Toby watched miserably. To make matters worse, he thought he could hear the cats meowing from somewhere outside the church. Maybe this hadn't been such a good idea after all. At last Uncle Tom finished preaching and walked back to sit with Toby's mother and father. He winked at Toby before sitting down in the pew.

When the regular minister stood up, it seemed to Toby that he was looking right at him.

The minister asked one of the men to dismiss the meeting and walked to the back of the church. Toby's feet twitched. Almost before the "Amen" sounded, Toby was out of the pew. He wasn't going to stand around for any questions. But at the door the minister's arm barred the way.

"Hold on, there, Tobias Lee!" he said, sniffing. "Just what do you have there?"

"J-just s-something for Uncle Tom." He pushed a cat away with his foot.

"For me?" said a voice.

Toby spun around, clutching his jacket.

There was Uncle Tom, a wide grin on his face. Mother and Father stood behind him. There were no grins on their faces as they looked at Toby's muddy clothes and torn jacket. Toby's heart sank.

Uncle Tom sniffed. "Why, Toby! You remembered how much I like fish." He reached into Toby's jacket and pulled out the wrapped fish. He unwrapped part of the paper and smiled. "It's your favorite kind, Reverend."

Mother stepped forward. "Why don't you join us for dinner, Reverend?" She glanced back at the grinning crowd behind them. "We'll cook Toby's fish, and you can visit with Tom, too."

"I'd be delighted." The minister smiled at Toby.

Toby let out a sigh of relief and followed Uncle Tom down the steps.

They hadn't gone far when Toby glanced back over his shoulder. Stretched out behind them were the town cats. Toby tugged on his uncle's coat sleeve and pointed.

Uncle Tom tipped back his head and laughed. "Toby, it looks like we're taking more than just the Reverend home for dinner today."

Glossary

This glossary has information about selected words found in this reader. You can find meanings of words as they are used in the stories. Certain unusual words such as foreign names are included so that you can pronounce them correctly when you read.

The pronunciation symbols below show how to pronounce each vowel and several of the less-familiar consonants.

ă	pat	ĕ	pet	îr	fierce
ā	pay	ē	be	ŏ	pot
âr	care	ĭ	pit	ō	go
ä	father	ī	pie	ô	paw, for, ball

oi	oil	ŭ	cut	zh	vision
o͞o	book	ûr	fur	ə	ago, item,
o͞o	boot	*th*	the		pencil, atom,
yo͞o	abuse	th	thin		circus
ou	out	hw	which	ər	butter

A **ac·knowl·edge** | ăk **nŏl´** ĭj | —*verb* To recognize the authority or position of.

ac·tu·al | ăk´ chōō əl | —*adjective* Existing in fact; real.

a·do·be | ə **dō´** bē | —*noun* Brick or bricks made of clay and straw that dry and harden in the sun.

adobe

al·ley | ăl´ ē | —*noun* A narrow street or passage between or behind buildings.

am·bush | ăm´ bōōsh´ | —*verb* To attack from a hidden position.

an·chor | ăng´ kər | —*verb* To hold in place; fix firmly.

alley

ap·proach | ə **prōch´** | —*verb* To come near or nearer to.

ar·mored truck | är´ mərd trŭk | —*noun* A vehicle covered with armor or some strong material such as steel; used for transporting money and valuable goods.

a·rouse | ə **rouz´** | —*verb* To stir up; excite.

armored truck

B **bail** | bāl | —*verb* To empty water from a boat.

bar·ri·cade | **băr´** ĭ kād´ | or | băr ĭ **kād´** | —*verb* To block off or prevent from moving.

ă	pat	ĕ	pet	îr	fierce	oi	oil	ŭ	cut	ə	ago,
ā	pay	ē	be	ŏ	pot	ōō	book	ûr	fur		item,
âr	care	ĭ	pit	ō	go	ōō	boot	*th*	the		pencil,
ä	father	ī	pie	ô	paw,	yōō	abuse	th	thin		atom,
					for	ou	out	hw	which		circus
								zh	vision	ər	butter

belfry

bay | bā | —*noun* A broad part of a sea or lake partly surrounded by land. —*adjective* Reddish brown.

bel•fry | běl´frē | —*noun* A tower or steeple where bells are hung.

bind | bīnd | —*verb* To wrap a bandage around.

black•smith | blăk´smĭth´ | —*noun* A person who makes things out of iron. A blacksmith heats the iron and shapes and hammers it into horseshoes, tools, and other objects.

blacksmith

bon•dage | bŏn´dĭj | —*noun* The condition of being a slave; slavery.

brief | brēf | —*adjective* Short in time or length.

bulk | bŭlk | —*noun* Great size, volume, or mass.

bur•ly | bŭr´lē | —*adjective* Heavy; strongly built; husky.

C **cane•brake** | kān´brāk´ | —*noun* A dense growth of cane.

canebrake

cane•stub•ble | kān stŭb´əl | —*noun* Short, stiff stalks left after cane has been cut.

cel•e•brate | sĕl´ə brāt´ | —*verb* To have a party or other festivity in honor of a special occasion.

chan•de•lier | shăn´ də lîr´ | —*noun* A light fixture with several arms or branches that hold light bulbs or candles. A chandelier hangs from the ceiling.

chief | chēf | —*noun* A person with the highest rank; a leader. —*adjective* 1. Highest in rank. 2. Most important; main.

cir•cuit rid•er | sûr´ kĭt rīd´ ər | —*noun* A preacher who traveled from church to church in some areas of the country.

circuit rider

clam•my | klăm´ ē | —*adjective* Damp, sticky, and usually cold.

clas•sics | klăs´ ĭks | —*noun* The writings of ancient Greece and Rome.

column

coax | kōks | —*verb* To try in a gentle or pleasant way to get a person or animal to do something.

cob•ble•stone | kŏb´ əl stōn´ | —*noun* A round stone once used to cover streets.

col•umn | kŏl´ əm | —*noun* 1. A long line of things or people following one behind the other. 2. A narrow vertical section of printed words on a page.

com•mu•ni•cate | kə myōo´ nĭ kāt´ | —*verb* To speak to; to pass along or exchange thoughts, ideas, or information.

ă pat	ĕ pet
ā pay	ē be
âr care	ĭ pit
ä father	ī pie
îr fierce	oi oil
ŏ pot	ŏŏ book
ō go	ōō boot
ô paw,	yōō abuse
for	ou out
ŭ cut	ə ago,
ûr fur	item,
th the	pencil,
th thin	atom,
hw which	circus
zh vision	ər butter

congregation

com•pa•ny | kŭm´ pə nē | —*noun* 1. A guest or guests. 2. A business; a firm.

con•gre•ga•tion | kŏng´ grə gā´ shən | —*noun* A group of people gathered together for religious worship.

coon•hound | kōōn´ hound´ | —*noun* A dog used for hunting raccoons.

coun•sel•or | koun´ sə lər | or | koun´ slər | —*noun* A person who advises or guides; adviser.

count•ess | koun´ tĭs | —*noun* 1. The wife of a count. 2. A woman with a rank equal to that of a count in her own right.

coonhound

cra•dle | krād´ l | —*verb* To hold closely.

cuff | kŭf | —*verb* To strike with the open hand; slap; hit.

D **de•lec•ta•ble** | dĭ lĕk´ tə bəl | —*adjective* Very enjoyable; delightful; delicious.

den | dĕn | —*noun* The home or shelter of a wild animal; a lair.

den

de•pend | dĭ pĕnd´ | —*verb* To be decided or determined.

de•pend•ent | dĭ pĕn´ dənt | —*adjective* Needing the help of someone or something else.

des•pair | dǐ **spâr´** | —*noun* Lack of all hope.

de•vice | dǐ **vīs´** | —*noun* Something that is made or used for a special purpose.

dodge | dǒj | —*verb* To avoid by moving quickly out of the way.

drought | drout | —*noun* A long period with little or no rain.

dry | drī | —*adjective* 1. Free from liquid or moisture. 2. Humorous in a clever or sarcastic way.

dug•out | **dǔg´** out´ | —*noun* A pit dug into the ground or on a hillside and used as a shelter.

E   **ease** | ēz | —*verb* To move slowly and carefully.

em•bank•ment | ĕm **bǎngk´** mənt | —*noun* A mound of earth or stone built up to hold back water or hold up a road.

es•cort | **ĕs´** kôrt´ | —*noun* One or more guards, often armed, traveling with a prisoner or important person.

ewe | yōo | —*noun* A female sheep.

ex•pect | ǐk **spĕkt´** | —*verb* To look for as likely to happen; foresee.

ă	pat	ĕ	pet
ā	pay	ē	be
âr	care	ĭ	pit
ä	father	ī	pie
îr	fierce	oi	oil
ŏ	pot	ŏŏ	book
ō	go	ōō	boot
ô	paw,	yōō	abuse
	for	ou	out
ŭ	cut	ə	ago,
ûr	fur		item,
th	the		pencil,
th	thin		atom,
hw	which		circus
zh	vision	ər	butter

ewe

filigree

ex•pe•di•tion | ĕk´ spĭ **dĭsh´** ən | —*noun* A long trip, usually for exploring or studying something not known or far away.

ex•pen•sive | ĭk **spĕn´** sĭv | —*adjective* Having a high price; costly.

F **fend** | fĕnd | —*verb* To turn away or aside; deflect.

fil•i•gree | fĭl´ ə grē´ | —*adjective* Decoration made from gold, silver, or other fine twisted wire.

flush | flŭsh | —*adjective* A blush or rosy glow.

for•ag•er | fôr´ ĭj ər | —*noun* A raider who searches or hunts for food and supplies.

G **ga•zette** | gĭ **zĕt´** | —*noun* A newspaper.

gin•ger•ly | jĭn´ jər lē | —*adverb* Carefully; delicately.

girth

girth | gûrth | —*noun* A strap securing a saddle on an animal's back; a cinch.

grade | grād | —*noun* A class or category; a type.

grav•el•ly | grăv´ əl lē | —*adjective* Having the quality of gravel; rough.

hearth

H **hearth** | härth | —*noun* The floor of a fireplace and the area around it.

hes•i•tate | hĕz´ ĭ tāt´ | —*verb* To pause in speaking or acting.

I **im•pul•sive** | ĭm pŭl´ sĭv | —*adjective* Inclined to act on a sudden urge, desire, or whim.

In•ca | ĭng´ kə | —*noun* A group of Native Americans who ruled Peru before the Spanish Conquest.

Inca

K **kiln** | kĭln | or | kĭl | —*noun* An oven or furnace used for hardening, drying, or burning such things as grain and lumber.

knead | nēd | —*verb* To mix and work a substance, such as dough or clay, by folding, pressing, or stretching it with the hands.

ă pat	ĕ pet
ā pay	ē be
âr care	ĭ pit
ä father	ī pie
îr fierce	oi oil
ŏ pot	ŏŏ book
ō go	ōō boot
ô paw,	yōō abuse
for	ou out
ŭ cut	ə ago,
ûr fur	item,
th the	pencil,
th thin	atom,
hw which	circus
zh vision	ər butter

L **li•lac** | lī´ lək | or | lī´ lŏk´ | or | lī´ lăk | —*noun* A garden shrub with clusters of fragrant purplish or white flowers.

loft | lŏft | —*noun* An open space under a roof; an attic.

lull | lŭl | —*verb* To cause to sleep or rest; soothe.

lux•u•ry | lŭg´ zhə rē | —*noun* Something that is not considered necessary but that gives great pleasure, enjoyment, or comfort.

loft

man•do•lin | **măn´** dl ĭn´ | —*noun* A stringed musical instrument that has a pear-shaped body and a long neck.

mite | mīt | —*noun* A very small animal placed in the same classification as spiders. Mites often live on plants or other animals.

mandolin

moat | mōt | —*noun* A wide, deep ditch, usually filled with water. In the Middle Ages a moat was dug around castles and towns to protect them from enemies. A bridge could be lowered over the moat so people could cross over it.

mol•las•ses | mə **lăs´** ĭz | —*noun* A thick, sweet syrup that is produced when sugar cane is made into sugar.

parchment

 nudge | nŭj | —*verb* To poke or push in a gentle way.

 oc•cu•pied | **ŏk´** yə pīd´ | —*adjective* Taken possession of and controlled by force.

out•ly•ing | **out´** lī ing | —*adjective* Located at a distance from the center or the main part; far away.

 pains•tak•ing•ly | **pānz´** tā´ kĭng lē | —*adverb* With great care; carefully.

parch•ment | **pärch´** mənt | —*noun* The skin of a sheep or goat, prepared as a material to write on.

pa•tron | pā´trən | —*noun* A person who regularly helps or supports a person or group by giving money.

per•se•cute | pûr´sĭ kyōōt´| —*verb* To cause to suffer, especially because of political or religious beliefs.

pinwheel

ă	pat	ĕ	pet
ā	pay	ē	be
âr	care	ĭ	pit
ä	father	ī	pie
îr	fierce	oi	oil
ŏ	pot	ōō	book
ō	go	ōō	boot
ô	paw,	yōō	abuse
	for	ou	out
ŭ	cut	ə	ago,
ûr	fur		item,
th	the		pencil,
th	thin		atom,
hw	which		circus
zh	vision	ər	butter

pin•wheel | pĭn´hwēl´| —*noun* A type of firework forming a spinning wheel of colored flames.

pi•rogue | pĭ rōg´| —*noun* A small boat carved from the trunk of a tree.

plan•ta•tion | plăn tā´shən | —*noun* A large farm or estate on which crops are grown and cared for by workers who also live on the farm.

port•a•ble | pôr´tə bəl | —*adjective* Easy to carry about.

por•ter |pôr´tər | —*noun* A person employed to carry goods or passengers.

porter

prance | prăns | —*verb* To rise on the hind legs and spring forward.

prey | prā | —*noun* An animal hunted or caught by another animal for food.

prow | prou | —*noun* The pointed front part of a ship or boat; bow.

prow

pulp | pŭlp | —*noun* The soft, juicy part of fruits and certain vegetables.

Q **quill pen** | kwĭl pĕn | —*noun* A writing pen that is made from a long, stiff feather.

R **ran•cid** | răn´sĭd | —*adjective* Stale; sour; having an offensive odor or flavor.

red•coat | rĕd´kōt | —*noun* A name for a British soldier during the American Revolution. The British soldiers wore bright red coats, making them easy targets for the colonists.

pulp

re•fuge | rĕf´yo͞oj | —*verb* Protection or shelter from danger.

re•gion | rē´jən | —*noun* Any large area of the earth's surface.

re•spon•si•bil•i•ty | rĭ spŏn´sə **bĭl´** ĭ tē | —*noun* Something that a person is reponsible for.

rus•tic | rŭs´tĭk | —*adjective* Simple; made of rough materials.

quill pen

S **scorn** | skôrn | —*verb* To treat someone or something as worthless or bad; look down on.

se•dan | sĭ dăn´ | —*noun* A type of portable enclosed chair for one person. It has poles on the front and the rear and is carried by two or more men.

sen•try | sĕn´trē | —*noun* A person who is posted to watch for attacks and to check people coming and going; a guard.

slave block | slāv blŏk | —*noun* A stand from which slaves were displayed and sold at a public auction.

so•ber | sŏ´bər | —*verb* To become serious; grave; solemn.

so•nar | sō´när´ | —*noun* A system that uses sound waves to discover and locate underwater objects.

spin•ner•et | spĭn´ə rĕt´ | —*noun* The part of a spider's body through which silky threads are produced.

squad | skwŏd | —*noun* A small group of soldiers brought together for work, drill, or combat.

sum•mons | sŭm´ənz | —*noun* An order for someone to appear somewhere or to do something.

thatched | thăcht | —*adjective* Covered with straw, reeds, or palm fronds.

thong | thông | —*noun* A thin strip of leather used to fasten something, such as a sandal.

ty•rant | tī´rənt | —*noun* A ruler who uses power unjustly or cruelly.

ă	pat	ĕ	pet
ā	pay	ē	be
âr	care	ĭ	pit
ä	father	ī	pie
îr	fierce	oi	oil
ŏ	pot	o͞o	book
ō	go	o͞o	boot
ô	paw,	yo͞o	abuse
	for	ou	out
ŭ	cut	ə	ago,
ûr	fur		item,
th	the		pencil
th	thin		atom,
hw	which		circus
zh	vision	ər	butter

thatched

thong

up•ris•ing | ŭp´rī zǐng | —*noun* A revolt or rebellion against authority.

vault | vôlt | —*noun* A room or compartment with strong walls and locks, used for keeping valuables safe.

vault

ven•dor | vĕn´dər | —*noun* A person who sells goods, sometimes from a cart on wheels; a salesman or peddler.

ves•sel | vĕs´əl | —*noun* A hollow container, such as a bowl, pitcher, jar, or tank, that can hold liquids.

vessel

vil•lain | vǐl´ən | —*noun* A person or story character who is wicked or evil.

wake | wāk | —*noun* The path of waves, ripples, or foam left in the water by a moving boat or ship.

wares | wârz | —*noun* Goods for sale.

wick•er | wǐk´ər | —*noun* Thin twigs or branches that bend easily. Wicker is used to make such things as baskets and light outdoor furniture.

wid•en | wīd´n | —*verb* To make or become wide or wider.

wicker

wist•ful | wǐst´fəl | —*adjective* Full of sad longing.

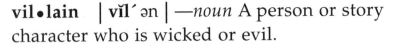

ă pat	ĕ pet	îr fierce	oi oil	ŭ cut	ə ago,
ā pay	ē be	ŏ pot	o͝o book	ûr fur	item,
âr care	ĭ pit	ō go	o͞o boot	*th* the	pencil,
ä father	ī pie	ô paw,	yo͞o abuse	th thin	atom,
		for	ou out	hw which	circus
				zh vision	ər butter